M000287997

The series 'Architectural Knowledge'
published by the Department of Architecture, ETH Zurich

Lloyd's 1:1

Michael Eidenbenz

Lloyd's 1:1
The Currency of the Architectural Mock-Up

gta Verlag

Preamble   6

Foreword   8

1. Mock-Ups: A Key to Problem Solving   12
    A Look into the Future   12
    Complexity in Building Design   17
    Lloyd's Building Design: Knowledge Work
    through Teamwork   18
    Book Structure   21

2. Starting the Dialogue   23
    Business Face-to-Face   23
    The Need for a New Building   26
    A Broad-Based Approach   28
    A Strategy for Lloyd's   33
    A Common Language   36

3. Visioning the Future   39
    The Megastructure   40
    The Intelligent Environment   44
    The Principle of Legibility   52
    Negotiating the Vision   53

4. Making Promises   55
    Establishing the Architectural Concept   56
    Engineering the Technical System   65
    Open Promises   118

5. Framing the Risk   **121**

    Management Contracting   122

    Planning the Investigation   128

6. Looking for Answers   **132**

    Shuttering the Beam Grid   133

    Assembling the Facade System   147

    Embossing the Structured Glass   163

    Ventilating the Facade Cavity   173

    Interior Ventilation   180

    Interior Lighting and Sprinkler System   182

    The Success of the Mock-Up Programme   186

7. Constructing Lloyd's   **189**

8. Mock-ups: The Currency of Experimenting   **206**

    Mock-Ups as Experiments   206

    Virtual Mock-Ups   209

    The Value of Architectural Mock-Ups   210

Bibliography   **212**

Image Credits   **216**

Acknowledgements   **218**

Preamble

There are surprisingly few studies about the role of one-to-one models, or mock-ups, in the building process. These full-scale simulations and their systematic categorisation and classification have hardly attracted the interest of building research, which instead tends to focus more on the development and use of digital simulation models to efficiently provide data for validating quantitative questions. Yet physically tangible criteria usually fall away with digital testing methods since they – at least for the time being – lack sensual experience.

Vitruvius describes in *De architectura* Book VI, 8, 10 (written between approximately 33 and 22 BCE) that anyone, not only architects, can judge what a good building is. But unlike the layperson, who only has an idea of the building when it stands finished, the architect, with only a mental image before having begun a building's execution, can have an idea of its beauty, convenience and propriety. Accordingly, the methods of architectural creation demand that something imaginary be transformed into well-formed and useful matter. To this end, architecture makes use of various instruments that are intended to mirror a later reality. One of these instruments is the architectural plan, which visualises buildings as a carrier and mediator of information. An exceptional early example is the St. Gall monastery plan, created in the first half of the ninth century, which demonstrates how that which is built in the mind is thematised, arranged and composed in a two-dimensional drawing. Subsequently, the instruments of architectural mediation, including the three-dimensional, full-scale model, have continuously been developed further. The role of mock-ups within this broad repertoire is not to be underestimated.

Michael Eidenbenz thus fills a research gap with his study. In his book, he interprets mock-ups, following Hans-Jörg Rheinberger, as experimental systems that are indispensable drivers for the further development of a building culture. Rightly so: the questions of promoting innovation, reducing costs, optimising schedules and increasing the quality of execution are still at the top of the building industry's agenda today, without relevant answers having been found so far. Fundamental questions revolve around the value, benefit and legitimacy of mock-ups within the planning and construction process and whether they enable the wide-ranging knowledge surrounding construction to be reacquired, coordinated and integrated in a new and informal way. Eidenbenz's study delves into these questions to show us to what extent mock-ups help to promote industrially usable innovations and their feasibility.

Insights gained from mock-ups link hard measurable scientific facts with human experience through observation. The case of the Lloyd's Building exemplifies a broad-based interaction of different competencies from natural science, engineering and architecture. Architects gain knowledge through observation which, supplemented by careful analysis and a precise understanding of processes, can re-dimension a problem's degree of complexity and make it more manageable. However, the long-standing model of the architects' sole control over the design process is broken here and replaced, as Richard Rogers often put it, by a community of practitioners. The thesis of this publication – that mock-ups bring to light the concrete and the realistic – is generated from this network of knowledge and information: a pertinent issue today as the digital dissolves our trust in the physical.

Already during the development phase, mock-ups help minimise risks in the construction process and later operations. Evaluating conclusions from mock-ups calls for an inductive approach. Observations supported by on-site measurements make it possible to record physical influences on an object. User behaviour can also be tested under real conditions. A trial procedure with mock-ups can therefore be used both to record effects of environmental influences and to shed light on the emotional human responses. Mock-up experiments systematically lead to usable, credible and convincing evidence. This methodology offers the possibility to draw concrete conclusions and identify effects specifically tailored to future users. However, it does not allow conclusions to be drawn about their causes.

Bruno Latour relativizes modern natural science's claim to objectivity and truth from a sociological point of view, thus bridging a seventeenth-century controversy between Robert Boyle's view that scientific experiment leads to the sole truth and his opponent Thomas Hobbes's rejection of knowledge solely based on human perception. Correspondingly, the mock-up combines purely scientific tests with the social dimension of a subject's confrontation with an object. Its three-dimensional, full-scale simulation convinces the client through facts, gives the planner certainty about the feasibility of what has been conceived and provides the contractor with information about the requirements of production and assembly on site. A revival of the use of mock-ups in architecture is due!

Zurich, May 2021
Sacha Menz

Foreword

Lloyd's 1:1 is the first thorough case study of an important twentieth-century building, but it is also much more. The exploration of the role of mock-ups in the construction process of this building opens new epistemological approaches in the analysis of architectural production and its permeation with the technical.

Until today, Leon Battista Alberti's paradigm (from *De re aedificatoria* I,1,2, which determines that architecture is created in the mind, expressed through drawings and models and then executed by others) forms the basic assumption for the profession of architecture in almost all parts of the world. But the original paradox in Alberti's paradigm has also entered the theory, and even more so the construction practice, of modern architecture: as Mario Carpo later put it, 'no construction drawing, no matter how rich, can ever hope to encapsulate *all* aspects of a physical object yet to be built' ('Craftsman to Draftsman', in Annette Spiro and David Ganzoni, eds., *The Working Drawing*, Zurich: Park Books, 2013: 279). However, the ontological gap he identified between the design intentions, their notation in the blueprints and their material realisation did not necessarily produce the architects' frustrations, improvisations, tribulations or intrigues; rather, the discerning representatives of this profession developed countless procedures to prevent the gap from becoming an abyss.

Carpo lists some specifications missing in the building plan that contribute to this gap: 'the door knobs, the Venetian blinds, the glass of the window panes, the colour of the carpets, the model and make of the electrical outlets' (ibid.). Some of these notational deficits can be compensated on a small scale: for example, carpet colours can be solved by using mood boards, a presentation technique able to evoke the mood and atmosphere of a room through haptic material presence and collage that has become indispensable in interior design competitions. At the other end of the spectrum, at full scale, is the mock-up used in architecture.

A look at the historical development shows that the scale model, such as a bozzetto or maquette (a first plastic formulation of two-dimensional design sketches in small format, usually for presentation purposes) has a long tradition in the visual arts. Alongside this intermediate state in the artistic process developed an appreciation of the model as an independent work with sometimes even a higher value than the executed object. The small-format design model was often followed by a full-scale execution model. For architecture, Jacques-François Blondel describes examples of such mock-ups in his six-volume *Cours d'architecture* (1771–1777; see the section on the usefulness of models for important buildings, including a wooden model of the colonnades of Gian Lorenzo Bernini's Piazza San Pietro in Rome). An early use of mock-ups in technical manufacturing processes is evidenced by visual and demonstration models in the aerospace industry and in industrial design, where the mock-ups were usually objects for various functional tests in which stress trials were combined with theoretical-scientific experiments. In the building industry, it was correspondingly the material testing institutes that promoted the experimentation with mock-ups as a method of research that understood the relationship between empirical investigation and conceptual-theoretical construction as both an interactive interplay and an iterative process.

In a discussion with architects on the question of whether architecture was evolving through experimentation, the designer Jean Prouvé attempted to demarcate technology from research by emphasising that constructing and producing technical objects requires acting based on technical determinations: 'You don't stand in front of a drawing board and tell yourself: "I'm going to make a house like this and that". ... On the contrary, I have always come to architecture by asking myself: "How could I make this construction?"' (quoted in Armelle Lavalou, ed., *Jean Prouvé par lui-même*, Paris: Éditions du Linteau, 2001: 136). He emphasised the intrinsic laws of the technical and posited that a technical determination is always polemical: it confirms or rejects a preconceived thesis by proving or disproving it, it creates a hierarchy of decisions, and in Prouvé's eyes it is precisely not the 'eternal' drawing that is expedient (at least in the industrial mode of production) but rather the prototype.

Accordingly, the long and tedious process of constructing buildings, unlike the private process of designing, takes place during an extensive cooperation between many participants. Michael Eidenbenz's work, which devotes an entire chapter to the project organisation of a highly technical building, logically begins with project planning with the chapter aptly titled 'Making Promises' before focussing on reducing and eliminating risks. The mock-up programme developed for this purpose reveals the diversity of this experimental environment: already after modelling and dimensioning the building's enormous open beam grid, the visible concrete surfaces of the megastructure provoked a systematic exploration of formwork techniques in different systems and mechanisms with yet more different surfaces and fasteners. This constructive and applied research activated all available knowledge, internationally and from numerous companies, to grasp the technical conditions for testing them in the mock-up. At the same time, however, the efforts had to outperform the available knowledge because the research demanded a twofold certainty for its readiness to experiment: first, the new object to be created was within the direct grasp of constructional rationality and therefore deserved the very name of the 'technically real'; and second, the tools and materials – especially the assembly technique of the formwork systems that had provoked the experiment – were already aspects of the experiment.

The construction of a mock-up as an experimental construction system has, to use François Jacob's words, the character of a 'game of possibilities' (*Le jeu des possibles*, Paris: Fayard, 1981). The comparisons and forced improvements in the repeatedly conducted mock-up experiment gave the architectural-technical thinking of the Lloyd's team a control function. Experiments could make the team of developers change their minds, a check that often created the need for further reviews and improvements of the systems – a process outlined in this book regarding the use of the Gleeson formwork system. Problems of a very different nature arose from the mock-up programme, such as ad hoc hypotheses, physical flow models of exhaust air windows or a structural glass with light bundling, are examined, all of which were integrated into the overarching research thesis of 'self-regulating membrane systems'.

The case study's central chapter shows how the mock-up arrangement disposes of, transports, verifies and extends largely existing technical objects in an experimental system. As a result, one of the most elaborate mock-ups in the history of architecture developed into an experimental setup in which it was actually possible to produce results that could be validated using complicated measuring instruments. Fritz Neumeyer detailed the architectural vision of a complete glass shell on the basis of the markings Ludwig Mies van der Rohe made in Siegfried Ebeling's 1926 *Der Raum als Membran* (Fritz Neumeyer, *Mies van der Rohe on the Building Art*, Cambridge, MA: MIT Press, 1991: 171–9), a vision that was reignited with Richard Buckminster Fuller's inspiration for Foster Associates' design for the Willis Faber & Dumas office building in Ipswich, a multi-level workspace enveloped in a light, climate-regulating skin, which was based on the idea of the 'intelligent environment'. The well-serviced shed, the recurring leitmotif of Richard Rogers Partnership and his like-minded colleagues, embodies the culmination of modern architecture's striving for a harmonious, technical coexistence of man and nature. This use-neutral, well-tempered space, in which overheating and cooling are in permanent osmotic balance, is still a focus of systematic research by climate engineers today. Particularly in the development of insulating glass with specific coatings and gas fillings, we can literally speak of a *tâtonnement*, a 'groping forward', as the French physiologist Claude Bernard explains with reference to his own experimentation (*Introduction à l'étude de la médecine expérimentale*, Paris: 1865).

The mock-up project for the Lloyd's Building took on almost monstrous dimensions due to the multitude of experimental arrangements. Countless elements came together in the experiments: combinatorics and statistics on light transmission and reflection, experimentation methods in the building physics of the ventilation of interstitial spaces, glass processing methods and their promising coating methods – elements that were otherwise largely dealt with in isolation at the time. Eidenbenz's analysis illuminates that the interior facade mock-up resulted in the modified system of an exhaust window with double-floor air supply and that, in coming closer to the ideal of the polyvalent wall, it was no longer the separation of building envelope and building services that determined the investigative arrangement. This integration of the air ducting into the facade construction also showed immediately, however, that the composite had left the power of emergence unexploited.

The history of mock-ups, as evidenced by Eidenbenz's excellent study, is only part of architecture and its history if one connects the use and purpose of mock-ups to the assumption that design does not precede technology, and if architectural historiography, like Cartesian science, admits the necessity of experimental testing – testing that has made mock-ups a mainstay of building technology and building culture to this day.

Zurich, May 2021
Markus Peter

1. Mock-Ups: A Key to Problem Solving

> Only with full-sized mock-ups can a client understand what
> a complex building design is all about.[1]
>
> Courtenay Blackmore, Head of Lloyd's Administration

This book is not about the Lloyd's Building itself. Rather, it is about the design process that enabled the construction of this London landmark. It specifically addresses the key role of mock-ups – real, full-sized models – that helped all involved parties minimise anticipated and unforeseen risks of this ambitious project. More generally, this book is about developing novel, buildable constructions, working as a team and solving complex design problems: all core elements of the design process of the Lloyd's Building in London.

The Lloyd's Building, designed and constructed between 1978 and 1986, provides an excellent object of study to show the potential of mock-ups. The late modernist building is considered an immensely ambitious project for its time, still designed with traditional methods just before the advent of the digital revolution. This book reconstructs the design process of the Lloyd's Building to show how the broad-based design team, led by Richard Rogers + Partners (RRP),[2] reduced the seemingly unsolvable complexity of their client's request to single, well-defined problems through an iterative, creative design process. In doing so, the team used the visionary ideas of megastructure and intelligent environment in a building design that relied on novel, yet undeveloped technical systems and constructions. To implement and validate the performance of these technical systems and constructions, the team collaborated with a managing contractor who built individual, selected parts of the building as full-scale models. These mock-ups allowed the team to settle remaining questions and ultimately minimize the risks of the building and its operations.

A Look into the Future

Mock-ups are models. As all models do, they provide 'a representation of a reality, where representation is the expression of certain relevant characteristics of the observed reality and where reality consists of the object or systems that exist, have existed or may exist.'[3] Yet unlike other models in architecture, mock-ups are real and true-to-scale models. The reality they represent is the future building.

Mock-ups are not new to architecture. Although historical remnants of such models are extremely rare, written sources indicate that mock-ups (by different names) have been used in architecture for a long time. For example, in his *Cours d'Architecture,* Jacques-François Blondel discusses such 'modèles de la grandeur de l'execution' and names architects who used them: Gian Lorenzo Bernini for the colonnades of St. Peter's Square in Rome, Pierre Lescot for one of the pavilions in the courtyard of the old Louvre, Claude Perrault for the Arc de Triomphe at the Porte Saint-Antoine in Paris and François Mansart for the facade of the Château de Maisons.[4] Until the middle of the nineteenth century, mock-ups were used only in isolated cases but from then on appeared more frequently because architects were increasingly losing control over the design of construction.[5]

Models help simplify a reality too complex to be comprehended or fully anticipated. Through this simplification, models reduce the complexity of reality and make it accessible for investigation. Models therefore can be distinguished by their level of abstraction: they focus only on a certain aspect of reality while abstracting the others. Like all models, mock-ups have the primary purpose of depicting something that does not yet exist by simplifying at least one of its aspects so that it can be examined and assessed. In most real models, the abstraction of reality takes place on the level of scale. Yet mock-ups reproduce dimensions on a one-to-one scale while instead abstracting things like the materiality, production process or the scope of the modelled reality. In particular, the ability to portray materiality at original size distinguishes mock-ups from the other types of models commonly used in architecture. The only difference to the real building is that the reality depicted by the mock-up is limited to a specific part of the building.

Like mock-ups, virtual models, such as building information models, can be accessed at a one-to-one scale – in fact at any scale – but they are not real. Industrial prototypes, although real and true to scale, abstract the industrial production of the serial product. The performance of the prototype is often identical with the designed product. But unlike the final product that is usually manufactured using automated processes, the prototype is instead produced by hand or by using digital prototyping methods (for example, 3-D printing).

Regardless of the chosen aspect of reality that a mock-up abstracts (be it the materiality, the production process or the scope), it can serve various purposes. In architecture generally, models – mock-ups included – can serve four purposes: description, exploration, prediction and evaluation.[6] Depending on whether a model serves other purposes, it can also be assigned to one or more of these four types. The descriptive model is the basic type of model used in architecture, from which the three other types are derived. It depicts an aspect of reality in such a way that it can be better understood by the observer. Purely descriptive architectural models are, for example, presentation or exhibition models. Apart from the description of a building, no other purpose is pursued. Among mock-ups, many facades created today for larger building projects (and probably most of the historical examples mentioned by Blondel) fall into this category. They reference the design and materialisation of a facade. They are used for demonstration (often for the client) and for quality assurance, and they can be revisited in case of construction defects.

Explorative models help discover new realities by means of variations through repeatedly modifying an originally descriptive model to assess new creations. Such working models are common in architecture, especially in scale form in early stages of design. The mock-up of Albert Speer's unbuilt Deutsches Stadion in the Hirschbach Valley north of Nuremberg is an example of an exploratory model in original size. The mock-up of the grandstand, probably unsurpassed in its dimensions, has the height of the valley flank and was built in two different variations to determine the optimal angle of inclination (1.01).

Predictive models are designed to anticipate values of measurable variables of things that do not yet exist. For example, predictive models are used to measure acoustics, luminous intensity, wind flow or load capacity. Predictive, full-scale models are known from the early days of structural analysis. In 1910, for example, Robert Maillart used an experimental model of his mushroom slab to determine the deflection (1.02). While physical scale models for measuring these quantities were common until the 1970s, the increased performance of computers is displacing them with mathematical models and simulations in practically all areas of engineering. Today, predictive mock-ups are usually substituted by simulations and are only used in cases where reality is not yet simulable – for example, in structural design when the behaviour of a node must be assessed in case of structural failure.

Finally, the evaluative model is used to assess aspects of a reality that are closely related but not contained in the model itself. Typically, these aspects are of a qualitative nature and therefore not measurable. They can only be experienced if the investigator relates the model to external information, for example by positioning it in a spatial context or by interacting with it by disassembling or assembling it. If supplementary information or interaction is missing, the model is purely descriptive. Evaluative models must be of

1.01 Albert Speer's explorative mock-up of the Deutsches Stadion to determine the angle of inclination of the grandstands, Hirschbachtal [1942?]
1.02 Robert Maillart's predictive mock-up mushroom slab to determine deflection, Zurich 1910

original size and thus are always mock-ups because any scaling distorts perception and interaction. Blondel, already aware of this deficiency of the scale model, noted:

> It is important to know that a small model never offers precisely the proportions that the large work will have: one must always expect to notice significant differences, because at a single glance, in the small model, one embraces the whole production; instead, in the building, one can only examine the parts one after the other.[7]

Evaluative mock-ups can be used during the design process to check the quality of interior and exterior spaces. For example, the mock-ups for Otto Wagner's unbuilt Kaiser Franz Josef-Stadtmuseum (1.03) or the Kröller-Müller House by Ludwig Mies van der Rohe (1.04) were installed at the

1.03 Otto Wagner's evaluative mock-up of the 'Kaiser Franz Josef-Stadtmuseum', Vienna 1909/1910

1.04 Ludwig Mies van der Rohe's evaluative mock-up of the Kröller-Müller House in wood and canvas, Otterlo 1912

intended building location. The altered quality of the urban or landscape space could be evaluated more reliably through the relationship between mock-up and context than by using a scale model of the situation. Another type of evaluative mock-ups is used for showing apartments built for marketing. By physically occupying the mock-up, potential buyers experience the interior qualities of the apartment. Finally, evaluative mock-ups are helpful for checking the production process when they are built primarily to analyse the process rather than the result.

Mock-ups, whether for describing, exploring, predicting or evaluating a future building, are applied in the design phase before construction work starts – from this viewpoint, they are design tools. They are, however, built by tradesmen who usually only become active in the construction phase of a building. This intermediary position between design and construction makes mock-ups an ideal tool for the collaboration of clients, designers and contractors. A mock-up forces them to apply all their available knowledge to make it reality. This not only includes formal, explicit knowledge but also informal, tacit knowledge. This form of knowledge is developed from direct experience. It cannot be expressed and is often perceived as a gut feeling: 'know-how' but not necessarily 'know-why'.

Much building knowledge, both in design and construction, is tacit. To solve complex problems, it needs to be exploited. With the help of mock-ups, the tacit knowledge of the involved parties can be made explicit and fed back into the design process. How mock-ups engage multiple parties to make various forms of knowledge explicit and implement them in the design process makes them a suitable tool for solving complex problems in building design.

Complexity in Building Design

Since the dawn of industrialisation, project complexity has been a major challenge for building design. Building culture, the collective knowledge of 'how things are done' struggles to keep up with the speed of social and technological progress. Often, solutions must be developed ad hoc or from scratch. This harbours risks because it tends to overcharge all involved parties, who then fail to deliver a robust building design. If building projects are not to become subject to contracting or liability issues and legal or political frameworks, these risks must be minimised through collective effort.

Complexity in building design is often driven by the growing number of demands that a building project must fulfil, including increasing expectations that insecurities or discomfort can be controlled by economic, political, legal, technical or aesthetic means. Two interlinked consequences have arisen from these changing demands: increasing regulation and a growing number of experts. Increasing regulation is expressed in laws, standards or specifications, for example those to ensure comfort (such as for lighting, heating or acoustics), protection (against structural collapse, fire, earthquakes or noise) profitability (through space efficiency, low construction costs and fast project delivery) or environmental protection (such as resource and energy consumption or carbon dioxide emissions). These regulations are represented by a growing number of experts who exert direct or

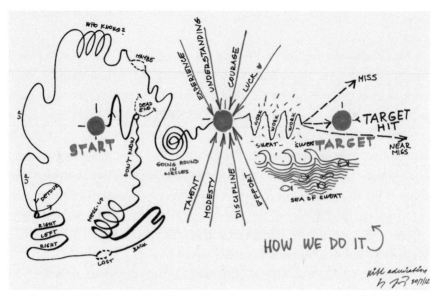

1.05 'How we do it'. Diagram by Eva Jiřičná, who worked on the design of the Lloyd's Building, illustrating the creative process in architecture

indirect influence on the design of a building project. The increasing regulation and number of experts results in numerous different but interdependent requirements, characteristic of any complex project.

The questions derived from linked requirements cannot be dealt with in isolation from one another since each answer in turn changes the framework conditions of other questions. (For example, the floor plan in an interior simultaneously determines the facade and the expression of a building, and vice versa.) Thus, if such requirements are treated as equivalent, derived questions can only be answered in their entirety. In building design, linked requirements are common. They are solved one at a time by changing one aspect and checking the others. In complex projects, this method of iteration may reach its limits due to the large number of linked questions and experts involved (1.05). Effective means of handling expert knowledge are therefore key to solving complex problems. Mock-ups, still today a relatively rarely used design tool, are worthwhile precisely because they are suitable for informally acquiring, coordinating and integrating the diverse (and especially the tacit) knowledge of all parties involved in design and construction.

Lloyd's Building Design: Knowledge Work through Teamwork
The Lloyd's Building (1.06, 1.07) is comparable in complexity to today's large-scale projects but was designed using traditional methods rather than digital design tools. While today it is mainly the extensive catalogue of requirements that leads to complex building designs, complexity in the Lloyd's Building design arose from the need to realise visionary architectural ideas

1.06 The Lloyd's Building by Richard Rogers + Partners, London 1978–1986

to fulfil the client's requirements. To tackle this complexity, a broad-based approach was applied that incorporated different forms of knowledge from a variety of experts working as team.

As a late modernist project, the Lloyd's Building is often classified as high-tech architecture, although the architect Richard Rogers rejected that term for his work.[8] Rogers and his team identified themselves less with the design vocabulary of this British architectural movement and its preference for using steel and glass but rather with its attitude to technology: in their eyes, the application and display of technology was not an end in itself but rather an expression of a functionalism that reflects the way a building is constructed and operated, not its use. The Lloyd's Building design principles, which aim to bring architectural and technical aesthetics into harmony, and its approaches to implementing the visionary ideas of the megastructure and the intelligent environment, express a culmination – if not *the* culmination – of late modernism. Or to put it in the words of Reyner Banham: 'Engineering is one way of designing things, architecture is another. The triumph of Lloyd's is, paradoxically, that it is so often difficult to tell them apart.'[9] Yet the path to this triumph was anything but easy with the high level of complexity involved. The strategy to overcome this complexity was to create dialogue among experts, as engineer Peter Rice explained:

> One of the most immediately striking features of the design is the way the technical functions are expressed and used in the architecture. For this to succeed at anything other than a superficial level the design must develop as a dialogue between the architect and engineer. The engineer cannot simply provide a technical response; he must understand the architectural objectives and take an active part in developing the concept of the building, in addition to solving the technical details.[10]

What Rice wrote about the engineer's work applied to everyone involved in the project. Viewing complexity as best solved by creativity, the RRP architects took a broad-based approach to tackle the challenges of the complex building design. In a team effort involving knowledge-holders from representatives of the client to the engineers and tradesmen, they analysed and solved the problems through creative dialogue and synthesised them in a holistic building design.

Creative thinking leads by definition to new approaches – be they aesthetic, constructive or technical – that need to be mature before moving from design to building construction. The team expanded during the design process to include a management contractor responsible for the administration and operation of construction work, which enabled it to engage for an extensive mock-up programme. This programme allowed them to include the knowledge of tradesmen to solve the remaining technical and constructive problems of the building design. Ultimately, the Lloyd's mock-ups allowed the clients, designers and engineers to take risks that were essential for solving complex design problems.

1.07 The central atrium in
the Lloyd's Building

This research shows that architectural mock-ups are not only models to assess the qualities of the future building. They also function as experiments to produce knowledge about reality – a feature no other design tools offer. Despite their high costs, they are invaluable tools for solving complex design problems but also important for research and drivers for progress in building culture.

Book Structure

After this introduction on mock-ups, complexity and teamwork, chapters two to seven are entirely devoted to the design process of the Lloyd's Building. To follow the iterative nature of this process, the structure of the case study does not follow the timeline but rather the logic of the design process with dedicated chapters.

The second chapter, 'Starting the Dialogue', introduces the client and the architectural practice: the Corporation of Lloyd's and RRP. It explains the needs of the client and the approach of both parties to solve problems through dialogue. Next, 'Visioning the Future' explains the origins and purposes of the visionary ideas of the megastructure, the intelligent environment and the design principle of legibility to which Rogers's team was committed. Chapter four, 'Making Promises', reconstructs the design process. It shows how the team around Rogers met the requirements of Lloyd's by implementing their visions in an architectural concept and the technical system, both harbouring the risk of constructive and technical (yet unresolved) questions. The fifth chapter, 'Framing the Risk', describes how risks were managed by taking two measures: expanding the team with a management contractor and launching a mock-up programme. Then, 'Looking for Answers' reconstructs the work on various mock-ups to show how mock-ups helped to solve not only well-known questions but also to reveal yet unknown problems. Chapter seven, 'Constructing Lloyd's', illustrates the construction process through images, while the concluding chapter explains how mock-ups are not limited to their purpose as models but also function as experiments. As such, they are still relevant for solving complex design problems today.

1   'Mock-Ups for Lloyd's', *Building* CCXLVII, no. 43 (1984), 20.
2   As of 1984, named Richard Rogers Partnership.
3   Marcial Echenique, 'Models: A Discussion', *Architectural Research and Teaching* 1, no. 1 (May 1970), 25.
4   Jacques-François Blondel, *Cours d'architecture: Ou traité de la décoration, distribution & construction des bâtiments*, vol. 4 (Paris: Desaint, 1773), 160–1.
5   Hans Reuther and Ekhart Berckenhagen, *Deutsche Architekturmodelle* (Berlin: Verlag für Kunstwissenschaften, 1994), 16–7.
6   For the typification of architectural models according to their purpose, cf. Nick Dunn, *Ecology of the Architectural Model* (Bern: Peter Lang, 2007) and Echenique, 'Models', respectively.
7   'Il faut même savoir qu'un modèle en petit, n'offre jamais précisément les proportions que comportera l'Ouvrage en grand: on doit s'attendre à remarquer toujours des différences sensibles; parce que d'une seul coup d'œil, dans le petit modèle, on embrasse toute la production; au lieu que, dans le Bâtiment, on ne peut examiner les parties que les unes après les autres'. Blondel, *Cours d'architecture, ou traité de la décoration, distribution & construction des bâtiments*, vol. 4 (Paris: Desaint, 1773), 159, translated by the author.
8   Cf. Peter Buchanan, 'Foster/Rogers: High-Tech: Classical/Gothic', *Architectural Review* 169, no. 1011 (May 1981), 265.
9   Reyner Banham, 'The Quality of Modernism', *Architectural Review* 180, no. 1076 (1986), 56.
10 Peter Rice and John Thornton, 'Lloyd's Redevelopment', *The Structural Engineer* 64A, no. 10 (1986), 266.

2. Starting the Dialogue

> I think the trend is toward architects working as generalists who work together or ideally bring in and coordinate a team of different specialists. ... The key word is teamwork.[1]
>
> Richard Rogers

The Corporation of Lloyd's,[2] a London-based institution that operates the oldest and one of the largest insurance markets in the world, had outgrown its building repeatedly by 1977. Lloyd's knew that the solution to its corporation's complex needs would require intense collaboration with an architect who would lead a team of specialists as a *primus inter pares*. To overcome its recurring lack of space once and for all, the corporation did not simply commission a new building but rather sought an architect who would understand its needs and with whom it could develop an enduring design that would constitute the dense and open atmosphere that enables underwriters and brokers of the Lloyd's market to conduct business by maintaining face-to-face interaction.

Successful projects in architecture often stand out by an equal dialogue between two partners. The selection of the future partner, therefore, was a key decision for Lloyd's. Richard Rogers + Partners (RRP)[3] was ultimately appointed to design and plan the new building, chosen because of the partners' compatibility in thinking and approaching the needs of the Lloyd's corporation. Lloyd's and the architects both worked under different business models but nonetheless maintained a similar approach for problem solving. The broad-based approach that RRP cultivated lent itself to the use of mock-ups later in the design process.

Business Face-to-Face

Lloyd's was established in the middle of the seventeenth century in Edward Lloyd's coffee house on Tower Street in the City of London.[4] As a place where shipowners, traders and venturers could meet, Lloyd's Coffee House not only provided guests with coffee, a new and coveted beverage at that time, it also offered the latest shipping information published in the paper *Lloyd's News*. Except for the Royal Exchange Assurance and the London Assurance, only private individuals were permitted to insure shipping risks at that time. Lloyd's Coffee House provided a place for establishing an informal trading exchange between private investors and traders.

As trade exchange in Lloyd's Coffee House grew rapidly, it became increasingly institutionalised, establishing rules, its own premises and organisational structures. Lloyd's developed a unique process for how insurance would be negotiated by facilitating the personal contact between all decision-makers and knowledge carriers through face-to-face business. This style of business has remained a unique selling point of the Lloyd's insurance market, one that even today continues to set Lloyd's apart from competing markets that are almost entirely electronic. Face-to-face business makes it possible for Lloyd's to quickly customise insurance solutions for complex risks.

Lloyd's became organised according to structures that still guide its operations today.[5] The Corporation of Lloyd's is operated by the Society of Lloyd's, whose individual members (the so-called Names), provide the capital for the market's financial basis. The corporation is responsible for the orderly operation of the market and its regulatory oversight. Staff members manage the properties and provide all other services for the smooth operation of the market, from errands to catering. The corporation, notably, owns the Lloyd's properties. The Corporation of Lloyd's can therefore be considered to have inherited Edward Lloyd's role: it provides services only and assumes no risks, which are instead assumed solely by its members. They are liable with their personal assets, which they pool to an unlimited extent with other members within syndicates. The so-called managing agents are the companies that manage these syndicates, for which they employ underwriters. The underwriters represent the interests of the members vis-à-vis the brokers, who in turn represent their clients' interests in insuring risks.

Lloyd's is known for its ability to insure odd or complex risks. In addition to the traditional segment of marine (shipping) insurance, the market also handles aviation, motor vehicle and non-marine (including liability and property) insurance. The spectrum of insured risks ranges from the loss of a particular body part to the failure of a satellite mission.

In concrete terms, a transaction on the Lloyd's market is conducted as follows.[6] Clients who want to insure a specific risk contact a broker certified for the Lloyd's market and explain their needs. The broker prepares a document with information on the subject matter of the insurance and the desired terms and conditions. And than walks – often on foot, as brokers working from nearby properties have done for centuries – to the trading desk in the hall simply known as 'the Room' in the Lloyd's Building (2.01a–b).

The Room is the heart of the market where the face-to-face business takes place. It is large enough to accommodate all the people involved in active

2.01 The Room: brokers (standing) discussing business with underwriters
(sitting) at the so-called boxes
a The Room in the new Lloyd's Building, 1986
b The Room in the old Lloyd's Building on Lime Street, 1978

trading, who establish a dense, buzzing atmosphere: at only 2.8 square
metres (thirty square feet) per person, the provided space[7] was ten times
smaller than the typical office workplace in around 1980.[8] The underwriters
sit close together on simple wooden benches called boxes. No specific work-
station is provided for the brokers, who circulate between the boxes to
converse with underwriters.

Each underwriter specialises in one market segment – marine, aviation,
motor or non-marine insurance. The broker submits the document to the

appropriate specialist underwriter and explains the client's concerns. In a short discussion lasting fifteen minutes on average, the broker informs the underwriter about the transaction and negotiates the insurance conditions.[9] The underwriter tries to assess the business risk by consulting – also face-to-face – various other specialists and then specifies the proportion of coverage his or her syndicate would assume in the event of a loss and the corresponding premium. With this information, the broker then obtains further offers from underwriters of other syndicates and contacts the client, who selects one of the options.

Since no syndicate provides full coverage, the insurance policy cannot yet be finalised at this point. Instead, the broker submits the offer of the selected underwriter (the so-called 'lead') to all Lloyd's underwriters, including those from other segments, under the same conditions. Only when the broker has been able to persuade enough underwriters to follow the lead (and thus provide full coverage) can the transaction be concluded. Every underwriter who follows a lead trusts the lead's expertise. The mutual trust among underwriters is the foundation on which business is conducted at Lloyd's. The dense, open atmosphere of the Room, which gives all participants an overview of the entire market, facilitates the establishment of contacts and personal exchange and thus promotes the building of trust among trading partners. The Lloyd's Room is thus crucial to the smooth flow of business.

The Need for a New Building

Although the high density of people in the Room of the Lloyd's Building was intended, the market grew so much that the limited space eventually hindered rather than encouraged the flow of business. In 1928, Lloyd's moved from the Royal Exchange (2.02) to a new building on Leadenhall Street but had to relocate to neighbouring Lime Street as early as 1958. Less than twenty years later, in June 1977, Lloyd's had to admit for the second time in fifty years that its new building was again too small.

Although Lloyd's was aware that only another new building could solve the space problems in the long term,[10] a solution to the lack of space in the Room was needed immediately. At the same time, uncertainty was growing about what impact electronic data processing (which was being introduced at that time) would have on the marketplace. Either a growth or a decline of the space required was thus conceivable.[11]

Lloyd's wanted to tackle its space problem for good and therefore sought a solution that would meet its needs over the next fifty years: in their own words, Lloyd's 'made two mistakes this century and do not intend to make

2.02 The Lloyd's insurance market in the Royal Exchange, where it was based until 1928

a third'.[12] In August 1977, Lloyd's contacted the Client's Advisory Service of RIBA, the Royal Institute of British Architects, for assistance in the search for an architect, particularly in organising competition procedures. However, Lloyd's was neither prepared to hand over decision-making authority to a jury, nor was it in a position to formulate its space allocation plan. The space problem was primarily of a logistical nature, so a project first would have to provide answers to the question of how to solve it.[13] Lloyd's summarised its requirements in six points, communicated in November 1977:

> Cater for the needs of the market for a period of at least 50 years whilst retaining a single Room by extensions and new buildings;
> Provide adequate space for ancillary activities and essential tenants in line with the expansion of the Room;
> Create a building of quality which not only contributes to the environment of the City but also maintains Lloyd's prominence as the centre of world insurance;
> Make optimum use of the land available allowing for a high degree of flexibility and choice of alternative strategies during design, construction and occupation of the building;
> Maintain full continuity of trading with minimum disturbance; [and]
> Develop a building which is generous in scale and quality but offers a highly efficient usage and keeps maintenance and overheads to a minimum.[14]

At a meeting between RIBA President Gordon Graham and Ian Findley, Chairman of Lloyd's, the latter proposed a selection procedure designed to evaluate a partner rather than a project.[15] The procedure was a novelty of its kind in the British architectural world: a selection of six architectural firms were to analyse the problems of Lloyd's and make proposals (for a compensation of ten thousand British pounds). These proposals were to be presented in interviews so that the potential future business partners could get to know each other.

Lloyd's was not convinced of the quality of contemporary British architecture and insisted on evaluating international architectural firms. The final selection consisted of I.M. Pei (based in the United States), Serete (in France), Webb Zerafa Menkes (in Canada) and Arup Associates, Foster Associates and Piano + Rogers Architects (all based in the United Kingdom), the latter of which would become Richard Rogers + Partners.[16]

The redevelopment committee,[17] composed of six Lloyd's Members and three senior Lloyd's staff executives under the chair of Sir Peter Green, invited all the participants to London on 8 November 1977 and explained the task. They were reminded several times that the task was not to design a building. The participants then were guided through the building, shown the Room and explained its importance for trading.[18] The event was concluded with an informal lunch which, according to Courtenay Blackmore, the head of administration and as such responsible for Lloyd's real estate, contributed to a 'colossal lowering of barriers'.[19] The architects were bid farewell with the task to 'set out in written and graphic form your appreciation of the problem, the overall approach you would expect to follow in developing a solution and arguments in support of your appointment.'[20]

A Broad-Based Approach

Piano + Rogers set themselves apart from the other architectural firms based on their strong commitment to a broad-based approach. Rogers had studied at the Architectural Association and Yale University from 1954 to 1962 and worked in different constellations (notably in Team 4, which he had founded in 1963 with his first wife, Sue Brumwell, and Wendy Cheesman and Norman Foster but which disbanded in 1967).

He began working with the Italian architect Renzo Piano as Piano + Rogers in 1970. Their first projects, which combined 'the London office's [Rogers's] interest in insulated, zipped-up skin technology and sociologically oriented research with Genoa's [Piano's] research into sophisticated, geometrical structures and thin membranes',[21] called for an inter- and

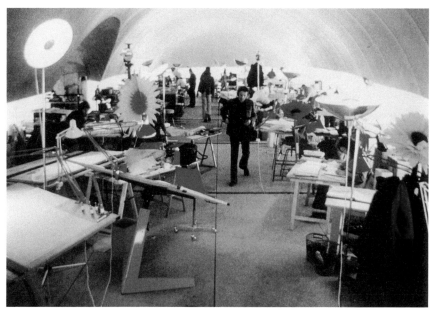

2.03 Common workspace of the design team for the Centre Beaubourg in a pneumatic structure, Paris 1972

transdisciplinary approach that would become a key element of the practice's design method. In 1971, they won the highly acclaimed competition for Centre Beaubourg (today the Centre Pompidou) and moved part of their office to Paris, where they erected an inflatable structure at the shore of the Seine that served as a common workspace for the architects of Piano + Rogers, the engineers of Ove Arup & Partners and the contractor Grand Travail de Marseille.[22] The proximity of the professionals and contractors enabled them to discuss complex design issues ad hoc (2.03).

The value of an interdisciplinary workplace revealed itself again in 1973, when Piano + Rogers were commissioned to design the research laboratories for Patscentre (PA Technical and Service Centre) in Hertfordshire. Patscentre, a department of the PA Management Consultants, developed products like components for music systems or home computers for companies that could not afford their own research and development department. Patscentre and its director Gordon Edge believed 'strongly in the important effect of the environment on innovation and creativity'.[23] Piano + Rogers therefore designed the laboratories to enable implicit communication between scientists and engineers and to 'provide the individual with an impression that he is aware of almost everything that is going on around him – the electronics engineer can see from his desk or bench that there is, for example, a sudden centre of interest around a project in chemistry.'[24]

The working environment at the Patscentre Laboratories and in the inflatable office for the Centre Beaubourg must have been in their minds when Rogers and Piano described their ideal successful collaboration in a manifesto-like text from 1975 as 'a broad-based approach consisting of individuals with different interests, strength and profession, living and working as a small community rather than the traditional vertically structured professional organisation. This group ideally works in the same space as the manufacturers, contractors and clients.'[25] Soon after, this idea of an inter- and transdisciplinary community would take concrete form in a new business alongside their architectural office.

Although Piano + Rogers had gained an international reputation by building the Centre Beaubourg, they received few new commissions after its completion in 1977. After Piano decided to return to Italy and drastically reduce his commitment to the group, the practice struggled. Still, it maintained a good relationship with Gordon Edge after the completion of the Patscentre laboratories and 'it seemed logical to pool our talents to attract new work'.[26] In an attempt to extend the practice's field of activity, the remaining team around Rogers started a new business with Patscentre under the name of Rogers Patscentre Architects[27] that would focus on technical research for the construction industry alongside the architectural office that, despite Piano's absence, continued to run under the name Piano + Rogers Architects (with the three partners Rogers, John Young and Marco Goldschmied) for publicity reasons until 1979. Only after Piano permanently left the group did Rogers formally reconstitute his office under the new name Richard Rogers + Partners (RRP) with his closest associates Young, Goldschmied and Mike Davies as partners.

Although Rogers later described Rogers Patscentre as the 'scientific arm of Richard Rogers Partnership'[28] 'in which architects and scientists work together to extend the limits of architecture',[29] this collaboration was more a platform for ideas and discussion. Nevertheless, it gave Rogers and his team direct access to engineers and increased their credibility within the construction industry, within which they could develop ideas for future architectural projects: under the name Rogers Patscentre Architects,

2.04 Micro 2000, the first digital micrometer, developed by PA Technology for Moor and Wright, the material, technological and architectural potential of glass-fibre reinforced cement

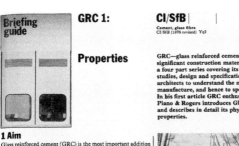

Briefing guide

GRC 1:

Properties

CI/SfB | | | Yq2 |

Cement, glass fibre
CI/SfB (1976 revised) Yq2

GRC—glass reinforced cement—is emerging as a significant construction material. This week we begin a four part series covering its properties, case studies, design and specification, which will enable architects to understand the nature of GRC and its manufacture, and hence to specify GRC components. In his first article GRC enthusiast JOHN YOUNG of Piano & Rogers introduces GRC and its manufacture, and describes in detail its physical and mechanical properties.

1 Aim

Glass reinforced cement (GRC) is the most important addition to the vocabulary of construction technology for years. The worldwide availability and comparatively low cost of the raw materials, and the relatively simple processes involved in the manufacture of finished components have triggered off widespread use of cement/glass fibre composites, very often as product replacements at the expense of traditional materials. By judicious selection of licensees and substantial investment in development and testing, Pilkington Brothers, the company vested with the commercial exploitation of glass fibre cement reinforcement, have fostered a sound base of reliability at a time when ever increasing demands are made on building performance, and when several other new materials have failed with disastrous results. Metaphorically speaking, GRC has emerged successfully from the crawling stage, confidently taken its first walking steps and in the next ten years should be running strongly in the mainstream of contemporary construction technology.

This series aims to enable architects to exploit the technical capabilities of the material in full and to develop a new language in the field of construction technology as GRC establishes itself as a building material in its own right.

2 Introduction

2.1 What is GRC?

GRC can be summarised as an ideal marriage between brittle materials, cement, sand and glass, to produce a tough composite. The principal ingredients are ordinary Portland cement, silica sand and water—the matrix—mixed with alkali-resistant glass fibres to produce the inorganic GRC composite. In the wet it has the appearance of hairy cement, 1. Because GRC is a new technology it is easy to forget that glass fibres are being added to sand and cement, not the other way round. Glass fibres constitute only about 5 per cent by volume of the material.

2.2 What are its characteristics?

The main virtues of cement are its low cost, its adaptability and its compressive strength. Its major disadvantages are its low tensile strength and brittleness. So reinforcing materials are introduced into the cement mix to carry tensile forces. The great advantage of cement reinforced with glass fibres is the ability to produce elements much thinner, typically 10 mm, and much lighter than is possible with traditional steel reinforcement where 25 mm or more concrete cover to the steel is essential as protection against corrosion. A little GRC goes a long way, 2.

GRC is inevitably similar to ordinary reinforced concrete in many ways, for example:
• weather resistance
• non combustibility

1 Cement/glass fibre composite enlarged about 50 times.

2 GRC canopies at a German petrol station.

2.05 Excerpt from a series of articles in which John Young examined the material, technological and architectural potential of glass-fibre reinforced cement, 1978

members of the practice carried out several research projects for manufacturers and suppliers, particularly in the period prior to the contract for the Lloyd's Building. For example, Davies was involved in the development of the first digital micrometer (2.04), Young investigated the potential of glass-fibre reinforced cement (2.05) for the Cemfil project for the leading British glass manufacturer Pilkington and Alan Stanton investigated future forms of the office for Knoll International (2.06). Finally, the Rogers Patscentre Architects authored the research study 'Notes on the Future of Glass' for Pilkington – presumably under the direction of Davies, who later was acknowledged as 'a former director of Rogers Patscentre'.[30]

Even though the business activity of Rogers Patscentre Architects lost importance after RRP's the commission for the Lloyd's Building, the practice held on to its problem-solving approach based on dialogue between a team

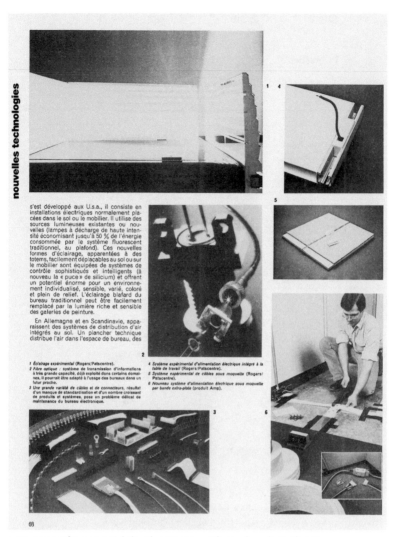

2.06 Excerpt from an article by Alan Stanton with novel products that Rogers Patscentre developed for Knoll International, 1981

of specialists in its architectural work: 'to keep up with science and technology ... our office calls together all the relevant specialists, including the consulting engineers, the moment we get a project. These engineers help to analyse the problem at a strategic level, in such a way that it gives us a handle on the architecture.' [31] The invitation to the selection process for the Lloyd's Building was not only an important opportunity to secure the future of the team around Rogers; it also allowed the team to prove the value of its broad-based approach in solving complex architectural problems like the one Lloyd's was facing.

A Strategy for Lloyd's

Despite its large appointment for building the Centre Beaubourg, Lloyd's considered Piano + Rogers inexperienced.[32] Piano and Rogers were invited to participate in the selection process for the new Lloyd's headquarters building because, in Gordon Graham's opinion, Rogers and Foster represented the best of British architecture.[33] To dispel Lloyd's doubts and to ensure expertise in the selection process, Rogers supplemented his team with specialists: Ove Arup & Partners provided structural engineering and mechanical services, Max Fordham + Partners contributed expertise in environmental physics and Monk + Dunstone Associates served as quantity surveyors. Engineer Peter Rice also played a special role. As a member of Ove Arup & Partners, he had already worked with Piano + Rogers on the Centre Beaubourg project. After its completion, he reduced his workload at Ove Arup & Partners to pursue other projects independently (with Piano and others). In the report presented to the Lloyd's redevelopment committee for the selection process, Rice is listed, before Ove Arup & Partners, as an independent consultant.[34]

In March 1978, Rogers's team contributed, per Lloyd's request, not a project design but rather a study that illuminated many different aspects of Lloyd's needs and thus also reflected the breadth of expertise in Rogers's team. The individual team members not only acted as specialists but also worked toward an overall solution. In addition to urban, energy and technical considerations, the study primarily explored the expansion potential of the property in outlining a growth strategy. Accordingly, in the introduction to the study, the team declared an open, adaptive system as the objective of the analysis:

> The aim is to define a system or strategy not a building. The system broadly allocates zones, defines movements and levels. Areas can change within this on an orderly basis guided by first principles. Sections, plans and elevations can change in answer to changing needs. The original pattern will be enriched by use.
> The strategy will define an open framework.[35]

Piano and Rogers gave only vague details about the shape of the new building in the report. Through a comparison of four possible building shapes (a tower (2.07a), slab (2.07b), perimeter scheme (2.07c) and deep plan (2.07d)), they concluded that a perimeter development around a central trading area would best meet Lloyd's specifications: it would provide numerous

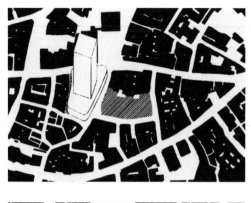

2.07 Four possible building forms to accommodate Lloyd's needs

a Tower
b Slab
c Perimeter scheme
d Deep plan

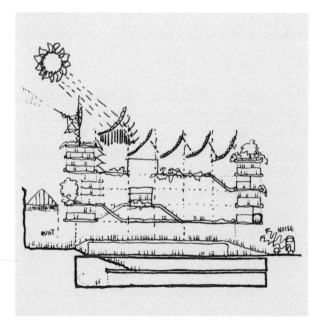

2.08 Concept sketch (section) by John Young illustrating suggestions for energy conservation of the perimeter scheme around the central Room, 1978

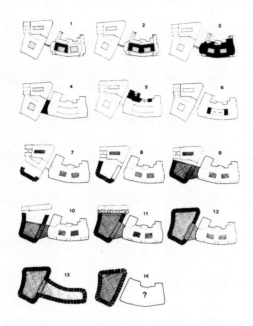

5. PHASING STRATEGY

5.1. Summary

The redevelopment strategy must, achieve two objectives:

.1. Allow the transition to be effortless and economical, retaining continuity of business at all times.

.2. Allow for changes in space requirements and occupation dates throughout the site operations.

Only if these two objectives can be fully met will the new development be fulfilling the brief.

5.2. Development Groups

The alternative development diagram nos.1-6 (Lloyds 1958 7-12 (Lloyds 1925 and Royal Mail House) and 13-14 (both sites) can be classed in five main groups.

Group 1 : provision of immediate additional 'Room' space within Lloyds 1958 coupled with temporary offices in Royal Mail House and no. 12 Leadenhall Street (diagrams 1-6).

Group 2 : provision for new offices fronting Leadenhall Place on the site of Lloyds 1925. (diagrams 7-8).

Group 3 : provision of up to 52,000 sq.ft. of 'Room' on the site of Lloyds 1925. (diagram 9).

Group 4 : demolition of all or part of Royal Mail House and no. 12 Leadenhall Street and provision for additional offices and potential room space for a total of between 413,000 and 509,000 sq.ft. (diagrams 10-12).

Group 5 : redevelopment of Lloyds 1958 site with a possible further extension of the Room. (diagrams 13-14).

These groups summarise in broad terms the possible strategies for redevelopment. Singly and collectively they offer Lloyds a range of choices with regard to both the timing and nature of the accommodation to be provided. Growth rates for the room and all ancillary spaces can be varied according to needs over the whole redevelopment programme.

5.3. Room Growth Options

Table 4 illustrates the potential for additional room space given by the implementation of particular stages together with the dates by which, at current growth rates, a renewed shortfall in Room space would occur.

It should be noted that the lower growth line B is simply additional space whilst the upper line A aggregates the existing 50,000 sq.ft. Room.

Thus it can be seen, for example that the implementation of diagram 11 provides Room space up to 2020 (if the present Room is retained for underwriting) or up to 1988 if it is not.

It must be emphasised that the diagram option stages are not fixed. They serve to illustrate the overall strategy. Further detailed study and consultation with the Lloyds community will determine a preferred phasing sequence.

Possible sequences based on present information could be:

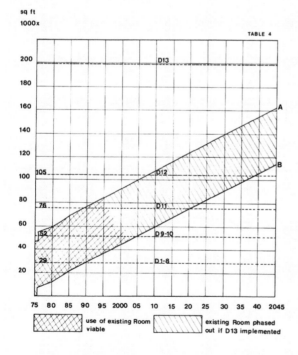

2.09 Phasing strategy, February 1978

a Possible interventions and stages of the redevelopment
b Potential space for the Room depending on the interventions and possible phasing sequence

35

advantages over the other building shapes, such as a good relationship to the townscape, efficient circulation and internal organisation of space, and long-term flexibility and 'virtually unlimited phasing potential'[36] while still using the available plot efficiently. Piano + Rogers recommended an eight- to twelve-storey block perimeter development oriented like an amoeba along the boundaries of the plot, entirely occupied by the Room (2.08).

The report continued with an analysis, backed up by calculations and graphs, in which Rogers's team compared various growth forecasts for Lloyd's with possible options for using the properties. An initial survey of the existing buildings had shown that they were inefficient, poorly lit and not extendible. Nevertheless, they did not obviate possible further use of the existing buildings, especially the building on Lime Street, because of the high cost of demolition and its high-quality finishing materials such as marble and stone. The analysis culminated in a collection of diagrams illustrating various measures to enlarge the building on Lime Street with additional floor space (2.09a). Piano + Rogers combined these measures together with the phased execution of the new building to create various development scenarios, thus fulfilling the promise of an open framework that would allow Lloyd's to grow in phases, whether in the short or long term (2.09b).

A Common Language
The interviews with the commissioned offices each lasted half a day, supplemented by an informal lunch. Rogers made every effort to maintain the impression that he managed an established and healthy company that had moved away from earlier avant-garde ambitions. For the briefing in November 1977, he bought a suit from Yves Saint Laurent and had Piano flown in from Genoa for the second presentation, thereby trying to dispel the rumour circulating of their separation.

The offices of Serete, Webb Zerafa Menkes, I.M. Pei and Foster Associates were dismissed from the selection in turn. The decisive argument against both Pei and Foster was difficulties in communication. Lloyd's doubted Pei's personal involvement given his domicile in the United States and his other commitments and worried that Foster wanted too much control. One Lloyd's member described the problem of the steep hierarchy in Foster's office by asking the question: 'What happens if his helicopter crashes?'[37]

After the second round of interviews, Lloyd's appointed Piano + Rogers Architects. Its strategy for Lloyd's and the well-founded analysis of the problems was the main reason for success. But Lloyd's also recognised that Rogers's team was the ideal partner for collaboration because it approached problems similarly and shared a common language. The compilation of the diagrams in which Rogers presented various possible interventions and stages (2.09a) was the key to building trust between the practice and Lloyd's: according to Blackmore, 'their fifteen sketches illustrating different aspects of the problem and how they might be resolved clearly reflected their sensitivity and the thought that each member of their team had given to the subject.' [38] The analogy of Rogers's 'small community' [39] to the Society of Lloyd's was obvious: like Lloyd's, Rogers was convinced that problem solutions must be based on a broad knowledge and experience base. This required a versatile, flatly organised team and, thanks to its proximity, constant dialogue. Following the same principle, new and complex business could be evaluated in the Room by collecting and evaluating possible loss scenarios in ad hoc discussions face-to-face with various experts. And Rogers's summary of the state of knowledge with the aphorism 'The one thing we know is that we don't know' [40] showed Lloyd's that his team had best understood the dilemma. [41]

Blackmore was extremely satisfied with the interview process. It gave Lloyd's insight into the different attitudes of the participants, their understanding of and approaches to the problems and their individual characters: 'The formula proved its worth since at the end the interview panel had a very clear idea of each practice's attitude and beliefs, comprehension of and approach to the problem, and the sort of people they were.' [42] This mutual appreciation of an open discussion culture undoubtedly allowed Rogers's team to enter quickly into a constructive dialogue with Lloyd's. Through the selection process, Lloyd's found not so much a solution to its problems as a partner with whom it could further develop the approaches outlined.

1   Richard Rogers, 'The Artist and the Scientist', in Deborah Gans, ed., *Bridging the Gap* (New York: Building Arts Forum; Van Nostrand Reinhold, 1991), 157–8.
2   The Corporation of Lloyd's, referred to in short simply as Lloyd's, should not be confused with the similarly named Lloyd's Register or Lloyd's Bank.
3   As of 1984, Richard Rogers Partnership; today, Rogers Stirk Harbour + Partners (RSHP).
4   On the history of the origins of Lloyd's, cf. Brian Appleyard, *The New Lloyd's: A Visitor's Guide* (London: Lloyd's of London, n.d.), 1–5; and Kenneth Powell, *Lloyd's Building* (London: Phaidon, 1994), 12–13.
5   On the organisation of Lloyd's, cf. Robert Ian Tricker, 'The Governance of Lloyd's of London', *Corporate Governance: An International Review* 1, no. 2 (1993): 84–92.
6   Cf. Paula Jarzabkowski, Gary Burke and Paul Spee, 'Constructing Spaces for Strategic Work: A Multimodal Perspective', *British Journal of Management* 26 (2015), 26–47; and Michael Smets et al., 'Reinsurance Trading in Lloyd's of London: Balancing Conflicting-Yet-Complementary Logics in Practice', *Academy of Management Journal* 58, no. 3 (2015), 932–70.

7 Cf. Piano + Rogers Architects, 'A Design Strategy for Lloyd's', February 1978, Archive RSHP, London, 16.
8 See Peter Murray, 'The Frontiers of Patronage', *RIBA Journal* 86, no. 9 (1979), 407.
9 Jarzabkowski, Burke and Spee, 'Constructing Spaces for Strategic Work', 45.
10 See Courtenay Blackmore, *The Client's Tale: The Role of the Client in Building Buildings* (London: RIBA, 1990), 110.
11 See Bryan Appleyard, *Richard Rogers: A Biography* (London: Faber & Faber, 1986), 236.
12 Quotation probably from Courtenay Blackmore, Head of Administration of Lloyd's; see Piano + Rogers Architects, 'A Design Strategy for Lloyd's', 2.
13 See Blackmore, *The Client's Tale*, 39, and Appleyard, *Richard Rogers*, 236.
14 Piano + Rogers Architects, 'A Design Strategy for Lloyd's'.
15 Blackmore, *The Client's Tale*, 39.
16 Appleyard, *Richard Rogers*, 236–7.
17 Cf. for the selection procedure Appleyard, 235–41; Blackmore, *The Client's Tale*, 39–40, Powell, *Lloyd's Building*, vols. 1, 13, 16; and Patrick Hannay, 'Two Politics of Patronage', *Architects' Journal* 184, no. 43 (1986), 53.
18 Appleyard, *Richard Rogers*, 238.
19 Courtenay Blackmore quotes from Murray, 'The Frontiers of Patronage', 405–6.
20 Piano + Rogers Architects, 'A Design Strategy for Lloyd's'.
21 Reyner Banham, 'Piano + Rogers' Architectural Method', *A+U* 66, no. 6 (1976), 65.
22 Cf. Peter Rawstorne, 'Piano + Rogers: Centre Beaubourg', *Architectural Design* XLII (July 1972), 407–10.
23 'PATSCentre International: Building Study', *Architects' Journal* 167, no. 26 (1978), 1248.
24 'PATSCentre International', 1248.
25 Renzo Piano and Richard Rogers, 'Piano + Rogers', *Architectural Design* 45, no. 5 (May 1975), 276.
26 Email from John Young, 12 December 2015.
27 Also 'Rogers PA Technology', cf. Royal Institute of British Architects, ed., *Architects '85: A Guide to RIBA Practices* (London: Royal Institute of British Architects, 1985).
28 Richard Rogers, 'Observation in Architecture' in Barbie Campbell Cole and Ruth Elias Rogers, eds., *Richard Rogers + Architects*, Architectural Monographs 10 (London: Academy Editions, 1985), 17.
29 'Architecture and the Programme: Lloyd's of London', *International Architect* 1, no. 3 (1980), 33.
30 Ted Stevens, 'Putting the Tech into Architecture', *New Scientist* 88, no. 1231 (1980), 705.
31 Rogers, 'The Artist and the Scientist', 139–40.
32 See Blackmore, *The Client's Tale*, 42.
33 See Appleyard, *Richard Rogers*, 236.
34 Piano + Rogers Architects, 'A Design Strategy for Lloyd's'.
35 Piano + Rogers Architects, 'A Design Strategy for Lloyd's', 2.
36 Piano + Rogers Architects, 'A Design Strategy for Lloyd's', 21.
37 See Appleyard, *Richard Rogers*, 238.
38 Blackmore, *The Client's Tale*, 40.
39 Cf. 'Architecture and the Programme', 33
40 Richard Rogers, quoted by Blackmore, *The Client's Tale*, 40.
41 Blackmore, *The Client's Tale*, 40.
42 Courtenay Blackmore quotations from 'Architecture and the Programme', 26.

3. Visioning the Future

There was no need for a detached avant-garde: time for that could not be wasted if the future was really to happen – now.[1]

Peter Cook

Rogers's team only marginally dealt with design issues in its winning contribution. Instead, it focussed on a development strategy for Lloyd's that would allow for spatial growth and supported its analysis with calculations of areas, statistics and diagrams. The Richard Rogers + Partners (RRP) team was aware that the pop-art aesthetic of its previous work, in particular the Centre Pompidou, did not correspond to the taste of an old, established institution like Lloyd's. Presumably for this reason, it avoided concrete architectural statements about the future building – a strategically apt decision, as Goldschmied's anecdote on the fringes of the jury's decision to award the contract makes clear:

> I was concentrating on having a pee when the Deputy Chairman came alongside to do the same. I concentrated harder and then he casually asked: 'Tell me, if you were appointed as architects for Lloyd's, it wouldn't look like Centre Pompidou – would it?' I clearly remember that reply too. It was 'Er … No!'[2]

Even if the Lloyd's Building did not inherit the colourfulness of the Centre Pompidou, RRP remained true to the ideas and principles that guided the design of the Centre Pompidou: the architectural ideas of megastructure and intelligent environment and the design principle of legibility. All three were shared by several architects around the world – and especially those in Britain – who propagandised for a change in architecture.

The architect Peter Cook aptly described the driving force and the role of the British key players of this worldwide movement, who not only envisioned a truly futuristic architecture but also did their best to make it real:

> Returning from America, some young English architects knew that they could and should make an architecture that was as the future – now. … Archigram emerged as the mouthpiece of this philosophy, Richard Rogers and Norman Foster emerged as its fashioners and engineers Peter Rice and Anthony Hunt emerged as its boffins.[3]

Although technology and society of the time (and still today) were not ready to make this futuristic vision fully come true, these architects relied on the ideas of the megastructure and the intelligent environment as the source of architectural concepts for their built projects. By doing so, they had to negotiate and eventually adapt these utopian ideas to the present conditions of technology and society, as RRP did on the Lloyd's Building.

In addition to the protagonists mentioned by Cook, the architectural historian and theorist Reyner Banham must also be attributed a significant role in the discourse of the time and in the formulation, specification and further development of those ideas. Banham, who had originally trained as a mechanical engineer, studied architectural history under Sigfried Giedion and Nikolaus Pevsner. As of 1952, he started working as assistant executive editor of the *Architectural Review* and later published influential works that addressed questions at the intersection between architecture and technology.[4] In doing so, he significantly influenced the ideas of the megastructure and intelligent environment. His articles and books not only reflect the avant-garde tendencies of the time but also embed them in the theoretical framework in which this group of British architects and the RRP team operated. While Archigram was, in Cook's words, the 'mouthpiece' [5] of that movement, Banham can be described as its promoter and chronicler.[6]

The Megastructure

In 1976 – one year before the launch of the Lloyd's redevelopment – Banham published a monograph that reviewed 'the great ongoing international megastructure conversation of the 1960s'.[7] To outline the idea of the megastructure that was encompassed by various regional movements such as Japanese metabolism, Dutch structuralism, British brutalism and Archigram, Banham referred to two definitions. The first one was from Japanese architect and Metabolist Fumihiko Maki, who coined the term 'mega-structure' in 1964 but only provided a vague description as a 'large frame in which all the functions of a city or part of a city are housed. It has been made possible by present day technology. In a sense it is a man-made feature of the landscape. It is like the great hill on which Italian towns were built.' [8] The second one by Ralph Wilcoxen from 1968 added clarification to Maki's description by depicting a megastructure

> not only [as] a structure of great size, but ... also a structure which is frequently: (1) constructed of modular units; (2) capable of great or even 'unlimited' extensions; (3) a structural framework into which

smaller structural units (for example, rooms, houses, or small buildings of other sorts) can be built – or even 'plugged-in' or 'clipped-on' after having been prefabricated elsewhere; (4) a structural framework expected to have a useful life much longer than that of the smaller units which it might support.[9]

Both definitions of a megastructure share the idea of a use-neutral supporting structural framework that can be adapted to the temporary needs of the users by adding units to it. Megastructures are thus characterised by a supporting structure that is not strictly designed for the requirements of a single defined use but can adapt to different purposes that change over time. Such a supporting structure is generously dimensioned, non-directional, changeable and thus very flexible.

In addition to Maki and Wilcoxen, Banham himself must be attributed to the development of the megastructure idea. Particularly in his contribution 'A Clip-On Architecture' for *Design Quarterly* in 1965,[10] he evolved the idea of an endless, adaptable and module-based architecture that soon became known as the megastructure in reference to the visionary designs of several other architects. In Banham's view, Alison and Peter Smithson's work on the 'House of the Future' (for the exhibition of the same name in 1956) marked the breakthrough of this idea of an 'endless architecture of indeterminate form'[11] that 'has been circulating in Britain for over fifteen years [since 1950]'.[12] Banham saw the novelty of this design less in the self-contained module for a house but rather in the town-planning proposition that

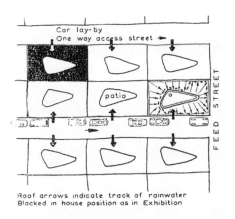

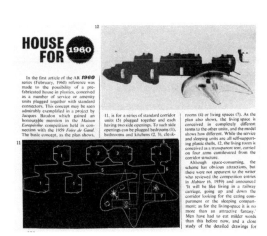

3.01 Town-planning pattern of the Houses of the Future. Multiple units are clipped together generating an endless mat-like arrangement. Published in *Municipal Journal*, March 1956.

3.02 Jacques Baudon's project for the Concours de la maison européenne. Excerpt from *Architectural Review*, April 1960.

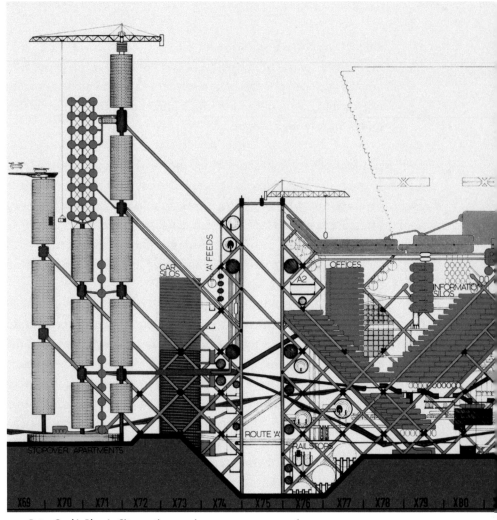

3.03 Peter Cook's Plug-In City, section, maximum pressure area, 1964

was part of the design (3.01). This single-storey development, made up of many units that were clipped together, represented the 'anonymous collective' Alison Smithson later identified as typical for mat-buildings – a flat type of megastructure.[13] The Smithsons' proposition, however groundbreaking it was, did not meet the challenges of high-density housing regarding how to build and service multiple storeys of such an accumulation of modules.

Banham attributed the first contribution to this conceptual problem to the Belgian architect Jacques Baudon.[14] With his entry for the 'Maison Européenne' competition in 1959, he proposed a concept for an infrastructure to connect many modules. In Baudon's project, the modules were no longer joined together back-to-back as in the Smithsons' mat-building but connected to a neutral structure. Each was assigned a specific use such as sleeping, cooking or bathing (3.02).[15] With this concept, the self-contained

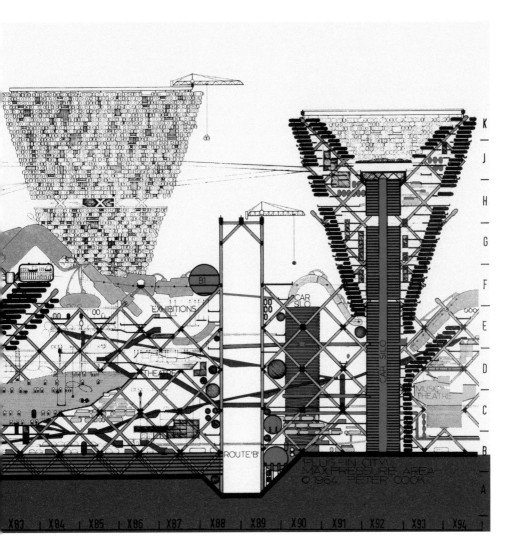

module developed away from the multifunctional habitat toward a specialised supplement to be 'clipped on' the neutral structure for an architectural
symbiosis.

As Banham showed in his article, the idea of a module-based architecture was further developed through utopian designs such as Archigram's
Plug-In City from 1964 (3.03). This project showed that the idea of the supplementary, technical module, clipped to a structure like an outboard motor to
functionally enhance it, could also be reversed. In *Plug-In City*, the structural framework provides not only static but also technical functionality: 'The
generalized structure becomes the source of power, service and support, and
the specialized clip-ons become the habitable units. ... like the connection
of domestic appliances to the house's electrical supply.'[16] This reversal of
supply and habitable units is why Archigram used the term plug-in instead
of clip-on for its urban projects.

While the clip-on concept solved the relationship between the supporting structure and building services by spatially differentiating the two elements, the plug-in concept integrated building services into the supporting
structure. To remain flexible, the structure needed to be not only expandable but also be highly permeable for the line routing of different media.
Both approaches make clear that a megastructure not only consists of an
undirected, expandable supporting structure and that its relationship to
building services engineering must also be clarified with this structure.

The idea of the megastructure absorbed several different concepts over
time. The projects, however, were not as radical as Archigram's utopian designs; most of them concentrated on individual aspects of the megastructure
idea. This also applies to the Lloyd's Building. Although it is not a megastructure in the strict sense of the word, as the structure was not designed to
be endlessly extendable, it exhibits many of the themes that preoccupied the
protagonists of that movement. Rogers was clearly committed to this idea:

> We see buildings, like cities, as flexible ever changing frameworks,
> which allow people freedom to do their own things in their own way
> – as giant erector sets rather than the traditional finite overscale doll-
> house which can be seen all around us, whether as glossy mile high
> office buildings or mass housing projects.[17]

The idea of a use-neutral, non-directional structure with integrated building
services, and the concept of clip-on units, had great influence on the architectural concept of the Lloyd's Building.

The Intelligent Environment
The idea of the intelligent environment developed during the same period
as the idea of the megastructure. It provided a complementary counterpart
to the megastructure because it addressed human needs for comfort that
the megastructure did not satisfy. Davies, partner at RRP, defined the idea
of an intelligent environment as 'a form of unified field theory of building
services where the building cladding, the building services and its information systems become one intelligent organism.'[18]

As in the article 'A Clip-On Architecture' from 1965, Banham again provided a key text to the discussion at the time with his article 'A Home Is Not
a House'.[19] Starting from the question of whether buildings are still justi-
fied at all in view of the dominance of building technology, he sketched out
an anti-structural vision of architecture: 'When your house contains such

a complex of piping, flues, ducts, wires, lights, inlets, outlets, ovens, sinks, refuse disposers, hi-fi reverberators, antennae, conduits, freezers, heaters – when it contains so many services that the hardware could stand up by itself without any assistance from the house, why have a house to hold it up?'[20]

Banham says these thoughts emerged from a flash of inspiration he had at the Southern Illinois University, where the architect and visionary Richard Buckminster Fuller taught at the time. Swimming at the campus beach – a place that in his opinion combined wilderness of nature and hygiene of civilisation in a typically American way – he caught sight of one of Fuller's lightweight, geodesic domes that were scattered around the campus, and it hit him that 'if dirty old Nature could be kept under the proper degree of control (sex left in, streptococci taken out) by other means, the United States would be happy to dispense with architecture and buildings altogether.'[21] Following this conclusion, Banham created the vision of an 'Environmental Bubble'. This combination of a mechanical device that supplied all elements for human comfort, and an enveloping, transparent, inflated bubble for minimal protection would allow humanity to assert its supremacy over nature wherever this unit could be placed.[22] Banham's vision became even more radical, merging these two elements – the mechanical device and protective bubble – into a so-called power membrane (3.04). The name is misleading because Banham's vision was not of a membrane but rather of a highly technical, umbrella-like device that generated a sensor-controlled curtain of warm air on the 'windward side of the un-house',[23] thereby constituting a 'warm dry lebensraum'.[24]

Shortly after Banham's article 'A Home Is Not a House', Davies started exploring the idea of a component capable of controlling the environment in a self-regulating way, in effect producing an intelligent environment. Unlike Banham, Davis did not focus on the apparatus that generates such a membrane but rather on the membrane itself. The article 'Pneu World' (a play on words with homophone 'new world') described a collection of pneumatic structures Davis compiled with fellow students of the Architectural Association.[25] In addition to several examples of these air-supported, mainly inflated systems, the compilation also included a description of a multilayer membrane by the German meteorologist and inventor Nikolaus Laing, presented at the first colloquium for pneumatic structures in 1967 (3.05).[26] Davies and his co-authors describe Laing's membrane as 'a multi-layer skin system incorporating heat-reflecting and heat-absorbing elements which can be dynamically controlled solely by air pressure. These regulate precisely air temperature, light, humidity, rainfall and air circulation, with solar

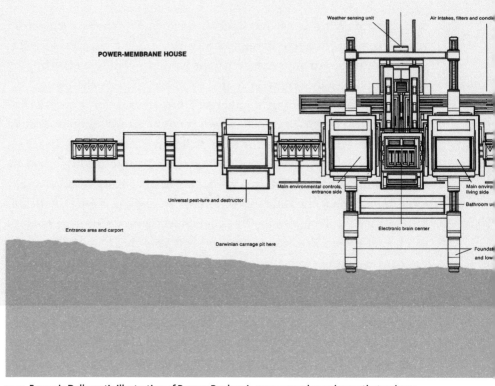

POWER-MEMBRANE HOUSE

Weather sensing unit

Air intakes, filters and condi

Main environmental controls,
entrance side

Main enviro
living side

Universal pest-lure and destructor

Bathroom ul

Entrance area and carport

Electronic brain center

Darwinian carnage pit here

Foundat
and low

3.04 François Dallegret's illustration of Reyner Banham's power membrane house that reduces the building envelope to an air curtain, 1965

radiation as the only energy input'.[27] Laing's vision of the membrane was ambiguously brought forth in the article titled 'Pneu World', which aligned with the promise that a world that uses the potential of pneumatic structures is indeed a new world – that is, one beyond the presently favoured regions: 'Tropical climates can be created in Newfoundland, and zero temperatures in the Sahara ... extending the human habitat beyond the presently favoured regions.'[28]

In the early 1970s, Davies began to experiment with dynamic pneumatic systems, such as his Light Mat (3.06), a system with which the passage of light could be controlled pneumatically. As a member of Chrysalis Architects, he produced the Pneudome, an inflatable structure for recreational use in California (3.07).[29] At the end of the 1970s, a research project for Pilkington Flat Glass Ltd. provided Davies the opportunity to further develop his vision of a dynamic membrane.[30]

Pilkington's main purpose in carrying out the study was to investigate the impact of new thermal insulation standards on glass products. It resulted in the report 'Notes on the Future of Glass', mostly devoted to the question of how the thermal insulation properties of its own existing product

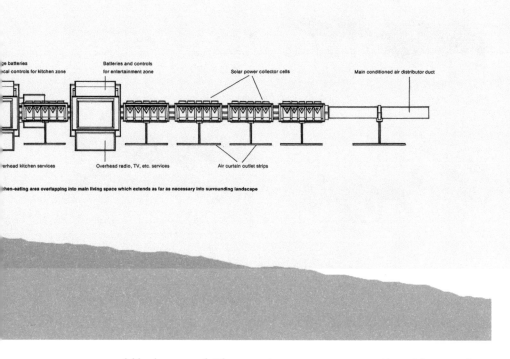

ge batteries
cal controls for kitchen zone

Batteries and controls
for entertainment zone

Solar power collector cells

Main conditioned air distributor duct

erhead kitchen services

Overhead radio, TV, etc. services

Air curtain outlet strips

then-eating area overlapping into main living space which extends as far as necessary into surrounding landscape

range could be improved. The report proposes, among other things, various fill materials for the product Armourclad, a sandwich element, which could be used to change not only the thermal insulation values but also the optical, static or acoustic properties of the elements. The last chapter of the study pointed the way forward for the idea of the intelligent environment in two parts, one regarding its design and the other concepts of responsive materials. Based on the conviction that the three factors of energy consumption, information technology and building automation would greatly enhance the technology and materiality of buildings in the coming decades, the report predicted a shift away from passive to dynamic climate systems: 'Buildings will effectively become "intelligent" mechanisms'.[31]

The report stated that controlling the indoor climate would require a continuous analytical tug-of-war between internal and external conditions. The antagonists here were the building's technology and its envelope: while the envelope separated the interior from the exterior, the technical equipment compensated for deviations from the desired ideal state by heating or cooling, humidifying or drying, lighting or shading. These technical devices were regulated by control loops with thermostats or photostats and by the active intervention of the users. They could thus react to changing conditions. Neither regulation by control loops nor by active intervention was ideal: the

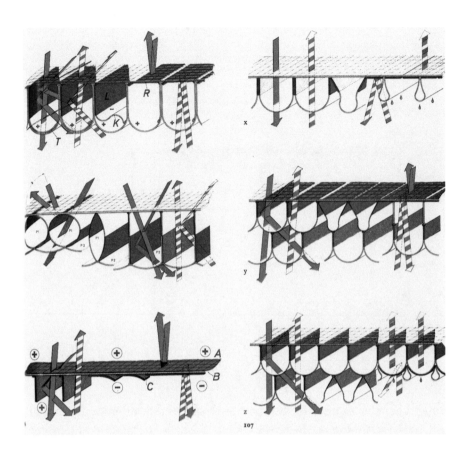

107

target value was often exceeded due to the high inertia of the control loop, and user interventions (such as ventilation) often acted in opposition to the automated system. Both cases resulted in an unnecessary consumption of energy.

The report did not state a fundamental problem with the control system but rather with the building's envelope: its physical properties (such as heat transfer and absorption) were static. Although they were usually optimised for a specific installation situation, once they have been determined, they could not be changed. The report recognised that improving physical properties (such as by increasing thermal insulation capacity) is not always effective: 'How does one increase the insulation of a window and still keep its other qualities. How does one let in solar energy, a significant energy gainer, whilst reducing glare and keeping insulative levels high?'[32] To overcome the widespread principle of building technology of hermetically separating the interior from the exterior with an envelope and controlling it with technical equipment, the report proposed a selective distribution of entropy between the interior and exterior environment. The means to achieve

48

3.05 Excerpt from the article 'Pneu World' showing the concept of Nikolaus Laing's pneumatically operated folding films for novel wall designs with radiation and transmission control, 1967/1968

3.06 Mike Davies with his light mat, a pneumatically operated light transmission control, 1971

3.07 The Pneudome by Chrysalis Architects, which included Mike Davies, 1972

this were no longer the envelope and the equipment but the selective membrane – the authors speak of a skin – inseparably connected to the organism of the building:

> The problem exists not because the external conditions such as sunshine level or temperature are varying, but because the boundary layers between the external environment and the internal environment are not effective enough as barriers to prevent some degree of energy transfer, in one direction or the other, through the building skin.[33]

A so-called responsive material, which required properties the report outlined briefly, was meant to solve this problem in the future.

In 1981, Davies published visionary ideas of the Pilkington study[34] and clarified the concept of a responsive material using the term 'polyvalent wall'. He illustrated his ideas with an exploded view (3.08) that showed the structure of a membrane of several layers, each a few nanometres thick. Each of these layers had a specific task based on an electrochemical or physical phenomenon. The polyvalent wall combined different effects like photochromism, piezoelectric photovoltaics and thermoelectricity in a dynamic, adaptive composite. The selective membrane was a key concept of the intelligent environment, as it could adapt to changing conditions inside and outside the building (3.09) to become fully functional by adaptively controlling the entropy distribution and the combination of membrane and apparatus in a complete system:

> We are faced with the prospect of intelligent buildings, with sensitive adaptive skins and internal energy distribution systems, monitored and controlled by interactive, high capacity microprocessors, capable of learning and incorporating preferences and habits of building users and local environmental conditions.[35]

Even though the technology and industrial processes had not progressed far enough in the early 1980s to realise the vision of the intelligent environment in the Lloyd's Building, Davies believed that a breakthrough was not far off: 'Much knowledge exists; it is really a question of the intelligent and creative combination of science and industry'.[36] This uncompromising belief in the future was characteristic of the attitude of Rogers's team and was evident in the design of the Lloyd's Building, in which the idea of the intelligent environment was always an important reference.

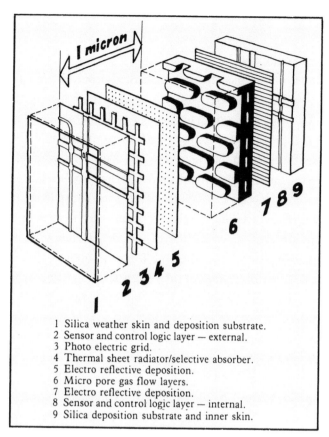

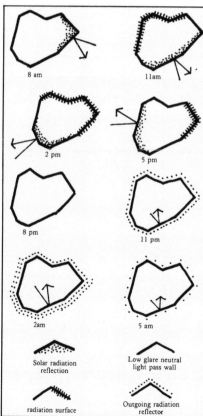

1 micron

1 Silica weather skin and deposition substrate.
2 Sensor and control logic layer — external.
3 Photo electric grid.
4 Thermal sheet radiator/selective absorber.
5 Electro reflective deposition.
6 Micro pore gas flow layers.
7 Electro reflective deposition.
8 Sensor and control logic layer — internal.
9 Silica deposition substrate and inner skin.

8 am

11am

2 pm

5 pm

8 pm

11 pm

2am

5 am

Solar radiation
reflection

Low glare neutral
light pass wall

radiation surface

Outgoing radiation
reflector

3.08 Exploded view drawing of the polyvalent wall: layers with different functions extend the performance of the envelope, 1981

3.09 The polyvalent wall responds to the changing solar radiation on a sunny spring day, 1981

The Principle of Legibility

The two architectural ideas of the megastructure and the intelligent environment were complemented by the architectural principle of legibility for the design of the Lloyd's Building. In contrast to an architectural idea that formulates a conception of a building, an architectural principle defines the rules according to which a building is designed. Thus, the principle of legibility regulated the mutual relationship between the whole and its parts: the building and its constructive and technical elements. It implied that, on the one hand, the essence of a building should be reflected in its elements. On the other hand, however, these elements were to articulate their constructive and technical function within the building as a whole.

Rogers stressed the important role of this principle in RRP's work on several occasions, stating that a legibly designed building should be understood by an ordinary person through a single fragment: anyone should be able to see from it how it was built and how it is used.[37] Rogers referred to ideas of legibility from Louis Kahn, among others:

> Each part clearly and joyfully proclaims its role in the totality. 'Let me tell you the part I am playing, how I am made and what each part does', what the building is for, what the role of the building is in the street, and the city.[38]

For Rogers, the principle of legibility had two benefits for architecture. As a construction principle, it simplified the later renewal or extension of the building since it considered the different lifetimes of the building components. As a design principle, it demonstrated the significance of technology. Rogers was convinced that 'technology cannot be an end in itself but must aim at solving long-term social and ecological problems'.[39] If this function of technology were displayed in architecture, it would furthermore enhance the aesthetic qualities of a building:

> To our practise its [technology's] natural functionalism has an intrinsic beauty. The aesthetic relationship between science and art has been poetically described by Horatio Greenough as: 'Beauty is the promise of function made sensuously pleasing.' It is science to the aid of the imagination.[40]

Rogers stressed that an architect who wants to plan legible architecture must understand the production processes of the individual parts and how they are joined together.[41] This requires not only an in-depth discussion with the producers of components but also with the engineers and the contractor. Rice shared this understanding and emphasised that, to express the striking ways in which the Lloyd's Building's technical functions, the design would have to be developed 'as a dialogue between the architect and engineer. The engineer cannot simply provide a technical response; he must understand the architectural objectives and take an active part in developing the concept of the building, in addition to solving the technical details.'[42]

Negotiating the Vision

RRP's vision of the Lloyd's Building was based on the ideas of the mega-structure and the intelligent environment. Together with the blunt display of the constructive and technical functions according to the principle of legibility, this led to radical architectural, technical concepts and a design language that were new for Lloyd's. Many of its Members were accustomed to traditional buildings and would need to warm to the prospect of working in a highly modern building. Negotiating RRP's vision with Lloyd's needs and expectations therefore went far beyond the issues of a typical building project. The ground for its success was already laid with the mutual trust between the two partners that was established during the selection process. The use of mock-ups would be another important key because they allowed RRP to bring its vision closer to reality and more clearly communicate it to the client by providing convincing models of the promised design.

1   Peter Cook, 'The Engineers Intervene', *The Architectural Review* CLXXIV, no. 1037 (1983), 49.
2   Richard Rogers, John Young and Marco Goldschmied, 'New Headquarters for Lloyd's', *RIBA Transactions* 4, no. 1 (1985), 52.
3   Cook, 'The Engineers Intervene', 49.
4   Reyner Banham, *Theory and Design in the First Machine Age* (London: Architectural Press, 1960); Reyner Banham, *New Brutalism: Ethic or Aesthetic?* (London: Architectural Press, 1966); Reyner Banham, *The Architecture of the Well-Tempered Environment* (London: Architectural Press, 1969).
5   Cook, 'The Engineers Intervene', 49.
6   For more about the roles of Banham and Archigram, cf. Nigel Whiteley, *Reyner Banham: Historian of the Immediate Future* (Cambridge, MA: MIT Press, 2002); Todd Gannon, *Reyner Banham and the Paradoxes of High Tech* (Los Angeles: Getty, 2017); Simon Sadler, *Archigram: Architecture Without Architecture* (Cambridge, MA: MIT Press, 2005).
7   Reyner Banham, *Megastructure: Urban Futures of the Recent Past* (London: Thames & Hudson, 1976), 6.
8   Fumihiko Maki, *Investigations in Collective Form* (St. Louis: The School of Architecture, Washington University, 1964), 8.
9   Ralph Wilcoxen, *A Short Bibliography on Megastructures* 66, Exchange Bibliography (Monticello: Council of Planning Librarians, 1968), 2.

10 Reyner Banham, 'A Clip-On Architecture', *Design Quarterly* 63 (1965), 2–30.
11 Banham, 'Clip-On Architecture', 8.
12 Banham, 'Clip-On Architecture', 5.
13 Alison Smithson, 'How to Recognize and Read Mat-Building', *Architectural Design* 44, no. 9 (1974), 573–90.
14 Banham, 'Clip-On Architecture', 9.
15 Cf. 'House for 1960', *Architectural Review* 127, no. 758 (1960), 223; and Jacques Baudon, 'Projet pour le concours de la maison européenne', *Techniques & ARCHITECTURE* 20, no. 1 (1959), 99.
16 Banham, 'Clip-On Architecture', 11.
17 Richard Rogers, 'Approach to Architecture', *RIBA Journal* 84, no. 1 (1977), 11–12.
18 Mike Davies, 'The Design of the Intelligent Environment', in *High-Tech Buildings* (London: Online Publications, 1986), 166.
19 Reyner Banham, 'A Home Is Not a House', *Art in America*, 2 (1965), 70–9.
20 Banham, 'A Home Is Not a House', 70.
21 Banham, 'A Home Is Not a House', 74.
22 Cf. figure captions Banham, 'A Home Is Not a House', 75.
23 Banham, 'A Home Is Not a House', 76.
24 Banham, 'A Home Is Not a House', 76.
25 Simon Conolly et al., 'Pneu World', *Architectural Design* 38, no. 6 (1968), 257–72.
26 Nikolaus Laing, 'The Use of Solar and Sky Radiation for Air Conditioning of Pneumatic Structures', in *Proceedings of the 1st International Colloquium on Pneumatic Structures* (Stuttgart: International Association for Shell Structures; Institut für Modellstatik, 1967), 163–77.
27 Conolly et al., 'Pneu World', 267.
28 Laing cited in Conolly et al., 'Pneu World', 267.
29 'The Bubble House: A Rising Market', *Playboy Magazine* 19, no. 4 (1972), 117–19.
30 Although the report attributes authorship to Rogers Patscentre Architects, it can be assumed that much, if not all, of the content can be attributed to Mike Davies.
31 Rogers Patscenter Architects, 'Notes on the Future of Glass', January 1979, Archive RSHP, London.
32 Rogers Patscenter Architects, 'Notes on the Future'.
33 Rogers Patscenter Architects, 'Notes on the Future'.
34 Mike Davies, 'A Wall for All Seasons', *RIBA Journal* 88, no. 2 (1981), 55–7.
35 Rogers Patscenter Architects, 'Notes on the Future'.
36 Davies, 'A Wall', 57.
37 Cf. Rogers, 'The Artist', 153.
38 Rogers, 'Observation in Architecture', 12.
39 Cf. Renzo Piano and Richard Rogers, 'Piano + Rogers', *A+U* 66, no. 6 (1976), 68–122.
40 Rogers, 'Observation in Architecture', 13.
41 Rogers, 'The Artist', 164.
42 Rice and Thornton, 'Lloyd's Redevelopment', 266.

4. Making Promises

Engineering is one way of designing things, architecture is another. The triumph of Lloyd's is, paradoxically, that it is so often difficult to tell them apart.[1]

Reyner Banham

In pursuing its futuristic visions, Rogers's team answered the demands of Lloyd's for a long-term solution of its problems with a building design that was rather an architectural promise than a technically mature construction. Although reports from Richard Rogers+Partners (RRP) on the outline proposal,[2] the scheme design[3] and later the detailed design[4] hold on to the clearly defined stages of the 'RIBA plan of work', the British standard for the organisation of the design and construction process of buildings, the design process of the new Lloyd's Building was largely characterised by iterative loops. Much back and forth exchange enabled the team to gradually shift the focus of the design from architectural to technical issues without having to deal with these two aspects of the design separately. Because architectural thinking influences the engineering of technical systems (such as the engineering influences the outlining of architectural concepts), teamwork was essential for such a design method. The team's broad-based approach allowed RRP to work in an integrated way where the different challenges of the design were constantly reviewed and revised by the relevant experts.

The benefit of this process that culminated in the scheme design was twofold. First, it allowed the team to converge the architectural concept with the technical system – two often conflicting aspects of a design. This resulted in an architectural construction that at the same time also expressed its technical functions and thus became 'legible' to passersby: a 'triumph', as Banham noted in the quotation above. Second, the complex problems of the task could be reduced from architectural to technical questions by transferring the visionary ideas of the megastructure and the intelligent design into a building design that would enable the Lloyd's insurance market to continue growing in the future. But although the team managed to tame these complex problems on an architectural level, the scheme design held a number of technical promises – and presented risks – that would have to be handled in later stages of the design.

Establishing the Architectural Concept

After being appointed to the project, RRP continued its constructive dialogue with Lloyd's to further develop the design strategy into a development strategy that met short- and long-term demands for the Lloyd's marketplace and established the principles for the architectural concept. The development strategy presented to and approved by the Members of Lloyd's in November 1978 condensed the phasing of the site development into a single stage, with the building typology of the atrium tower and a spatial concept of clear span floors served by attached elements.[5] This starting point of the architectural concept that defined the spatial zoning and circulation of the new building was later further developed in an iterative process alongside the technical system, lastly resulting in the detailed design.[6]

Phasing

RRP's design strategy for Lloyd's culminated in a collection of diagrams illustrating various measures to gain additional floor area (2.09a).[7] Since the acute lack of space in the old Room had been the trigger for the Lloyd's redevelopment, RRP, besides proposing several measurements for a new building, also paid special attention to the existing one. A combination of these options in the design strategy led to several developments that differed in extents, sequence and phasing.

As medium-term remedies for the lack of space in the old Room, RRP proposed to convert an underground car park and telephone centre in the basement of the existing building and extend the Room's gallery.[8] For the Room to be able to absorb the growth of the market in the longer term – Lloyd's target was the next fifty years – the site across Lime Street on Leadenhall Street would also need to be included in the expansion. On this site was the former Royal Post Office, a listed building that had housed the Lloyd's Room from 1928–1958. Only after negotiations did the authorities allow the demolition of the Royal Post Office on the condition that the entrance portal be retained.

RRP examined two options for the development of this site: a two-stage development (4.01a) in which the Room would be extended to the existing building across Lime Street by two phases of extensions on the vacant lot; and a single-stage development (4.01b), which would provide for a new detached building on the vacant lot. Under the single-stage development plan, the new building would eventually replace the old one and free it for further rental. An analysis of the two options showed that implementing the growth strategy in one step had several advantages over a two-step approach: not

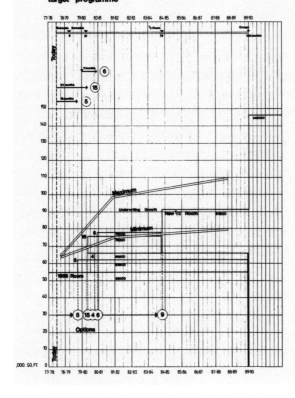

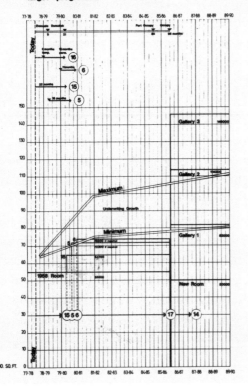

4.01 Development strategies, October 1978

a Two-stage development

b Single-stage development

only would it be cheaper and faster overall, single-stage development would allow the marketplace to continue operating in the old premises without disruption during construction work until the relocation of the market in the new building – an extremely important criterion for Lloyd's.[9] But using a single-step development approach on a multi-storey building would introduce challenges to a coherent marketplace spread over several floors.

In addition to these economic and organisational advantages, the single-stage option would also bring a change new to Lloyd's spatial growth strategy: instead of enlarging the width of the Room horizontally on the ground floor, as previously planned, the long-term expansion in the new detached building would take place vertically by stacked floors. This development strategy was common for inner-city office spaces but new and challenging for a stock exchange like Lloyd's, and it would have far-reaching consequences for the typology and spatial concept of the new building.

Typology and space

The face-to-face business conducted at Lloyd's differed from how a typical office would use space, which placed special demands on a building with stacked floors. Firstly, a visual reference would be needed within and across the floors to ensure the unity of the market. Secondly, the floors themselves would have to be designed in such a way that they could accommodate a significantly higher density of people than that of an office building. Because a conventional multi-storey building would not be able to meet these requirements, a new kind of typology and spatial concept was necessary.

The historical typology for trade buildings, such as in marketplaces or stock exchanges, is the hall. Prominent examples for this building type include the Royal Exchange in London or the Beurs van Berlage in Amsterdam but also nineteenth-century department stores such as the Grands Magasins du Louvre in Paris. The old Room of Lloyd's at Lime Street was also a hall. The central, two-storey high room where most of the trade was conducted was illuminated by large skylights. Only a small part of the usable space was on the narrow gallery of the upper floor.

RRP proposed a multi-storey building with an integrated atrium that would create 'a series of galleries around the main floor of the Room capable of accommodating a growth in underwriting space to 150,000 square feet or more whilst maintaining a single market both functionally and visually'.[10] A revived typology of the atrium tower would guarantee the unity of the Room by enabling visual contact between the underwriters and the brokers on the different market floors, thus allowing the smooth flow of

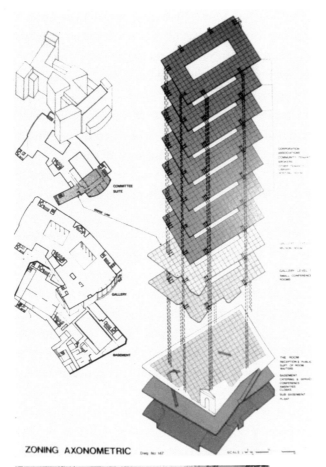

ZONING AXONOMETRIC

4.02 Axonometric showing typology, spatial zoning, access and circulation, October 1978

4.03 Example of an early atrium tower: Chamber of Commerce Building by Baumann and Huehl, Chicago 1890. The so-called 'light well' ventilates and illuminates the deep floor plan.

business (4.02). Although the atrium tower can be interpreted as an upwardly extended variation of the hall, these two typologies are based on different intentions. While the hall protected the open marketplace from the weather, an atrium would supply deep floor plans with light and air. It originated in early buildings of the Chicago School, where the supply of daylight to the offices was an important usage criterion (4.03).[11] These so-called light wells may also have been the model for Frank Lloyd Wright's Larkin Building in Buffalo, New York, which made the office building atrium typology known worldwide. Banham, moreover, demonstrated the importance of this building typology for the development of air conditioning technology on several occasions.[12]

Due to increasing electrification and mechanical air conditioning of office buildings, however, the typology of the atrium tower lost its purpose around 1900. Deep floors with tightly furnished open-plan offices (and, since the end of the 1950s, organic *Bürolandschaften*) began to dominate the working environment. It was not until the 1970s that the interest in atriums began to grow again. Buildings such as the 1972 Centraal Beheer Verwaltung by Herman Hertzberger showed how the generous vertical interiors of atriums could interrupt the monotonous working environment of open-plan offices and create energy-efficient solutions.[13]

Paradoxically, the atrium, while strengthening the unity of the Room by interlinking the different floors, also threatened this important feature. The empty space of the atrium reduced the floor space by around twenty per cent, creating an even smaller floor that was already diminished by the large number of toilets, lifts and escape stairs that were required because of the high density of people in the Room (4.04a). Although this space could be reclaimed with additional upper floors because building regulations did not stipulate a maximum building height, each of these additional floors would result in brokers walking longer distances, thus weakening the unity of the Room and hindering the flow of trade.

RRP solved this paradox by arranging all the servant elements (the circulation, ancillary rooms, main lines of the building services and structure columns) outside the main volume, which created free open floors with a maximum continuous usable area (4.04b). These floors could not only be arbitrarily adapted to the respective use (office or market) but also allowed for the highest concentration of trading space near the ground floor. To further reduce the long walking distances within the Room, RRP placed intersecting escalators in the otherwise empty atrium, following an approach that was first used in American shopping centres.[14]

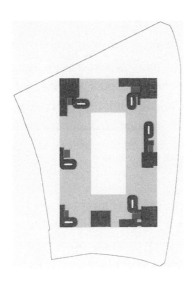
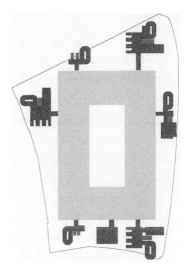

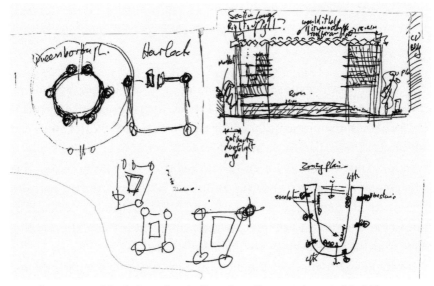

4.04a–b Diagrams of the design to free the floors from all servant elements (blue). These are arranged as clip-ons in the satellite towers around the main building that holds only the Room (yellow).

4.05 Early design sketches including medieval fortresses, perimeter scheme and U-shaped zoning plan, Richard Rogers

A sketch by Rogers shows that the outer placement of the circulation was already considered in an early, U-shaped variant of the building following a scheme already applied at the Centre Pompidou (4.05). RRP went even further at the Lloyd's Building by placing all vertical elements outside the building. Additional sketches on the same sheet show the plans of the medieval fortresses of Queensborough and Harlech, whose dominant fortified towers must have inspired RRP to distribute these outer elements not, as in the Centre Pompidou, evenly along the facade, but rather to bundle them into six so-called satellite towers. In addition to medieval fortresses, RRP must have drawn inspiration from the striking towers of Louis Kahn's 1960 Richards Medical Research Laboratories in Philadelphia. In contrast to Kahn's abstract, uniform towers, however, RRP articulated the constructive and technical functions of the structural elements and the services, taking Banham's criticism of Kahn's building to heart (4.06):

> Kahn has dramatized the fact that his building is mechanically ser- viced, but he seems to be pretty insensitive to the nature and func- tions of those services. ... there is an element of falsehood in making the expression of services as monumental and ponderous as Kahn has done. The theme is not a fit one for monumentality, but we have not yet reached a sufficient state of self-confident ease in our tech- nological environment to be able to take services quietly on the out- side of a building.[15]

While the way in which the satellite towers are arranged around the building can be traced back to the Richards Medical Research Laboratories and medi- eval fortresses, their expression is oriented toward Kisho Kurokawa's cap- sule projects in Tokyo. His Nagakin Capsule Tower from 1972, and especial- ly the Sony Tower from 1976, seem to have been not only conceptual but also iconographic references for RRP (4.07). An early RRP drawing of the capsules for the satellite towers shows obvious similarities to the ones designed by Kurokawa for the Sony Tower in the twin porthole windows and the cladding made from the same deep-drawn metal sheets (4.45).

The large and connected usable area that was gained by freeing the floors from servant elements would not only strengthen the unity of the Room but would also allow future changes to its use. Lloyd's expected that the market would occupy two galleries and the ground floor once completed. For later growth, up to three additional galleries could be added by transforming of- fice space to trading floors (4.08).

While complying with Lloyd's needs, the proposed typology and spatial concept at the same time reflected RRP's commitment to the ideas of the megastructure, the intelligent environment and the principle of legibility. The outer placement of the servant elements and the structure made their assembly and function visible and therefore legible to everyday passersby. The articulation and hierarchy of joining those elements followed the differ- ent life span of the individual elements, allowing for easy replacement throughout the life cycle of the building. In the logic of the megastructure,

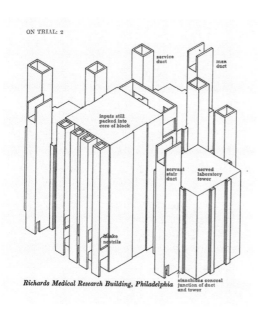

4.06 Diagram of the Richards Medical Research Laboratories by Louis Kahn

4.07 Sony tower by Kisho Kurokawa including toilet capsules with twin porthole windows, Osaka 1976

63

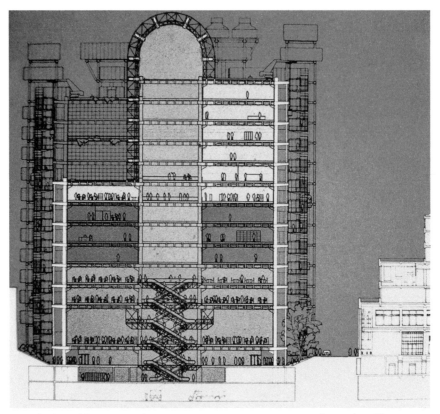

4.08 Lloyd's Building, section showing usage options. Orange areas can be used as offices or added later to the Room.

these outer elements are clip-ons that provide the main building with technical infrastructure. The proposed spatial concept for the main building, 'a highly adaptable clear span series of floors giving a highly efficient space suitable both for Lloyd's underwriting and for prime lettable office space throughout the life of the building',[16] was later labelled as the Omniplatz by the architectural critic Colin Davies.[17] This neologism derived from the Latin-based prefix *omni-* (everything/all/universal) and the German *Arbeitsplatz* (workplace) aptly described the seemingly endless, homogeneous and comfortable space with a maximum surface area, optimised energy consumption and articulated construction and technology – all aspects which RRP promised to turn the idea of an intelligent environment into reality (4.09).

At an extraordinary meeting in November 1978, a large majority of 83 per cent of the Lloyd's Members adopted the development strategy. Even though the typology of the atrium tower and the concept of a homogeneous, adaptable space promised a contemporary solution for Lloyd's needs, the ambitious strategy posed several risks. The offer to provide a long-term solution

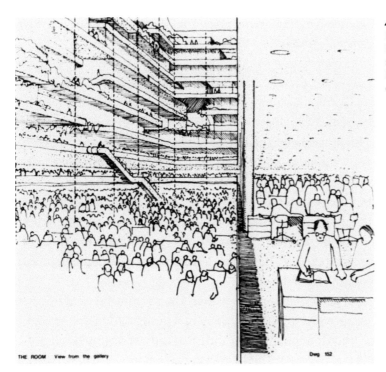

4.09 View of the Room from a gallery illustrating the seemingly endless, homogeneous and comfortable space

to Lloyd's growing space requirements by building a highly efficient and adaptable space whose area could be used down to the last square metre was merely a promise for the time being. The technical systems that were required to construct and service such a space still had to be clarified.

Engineering the Technical System

RRP presented the typological and spatial concept to the Members of Lloyd's in the development strategy of November 1978, which determined the new building's spatial zoning and circulation. In the further course of design, systems would have to be developed in response to technical demands raised by the typology and the spatial concept. These included the air conditioning technology, the main structure, the building envelope and the service towers with capsules, lifts and emergency staircases. The various elements not only had to be materialised and dimensioned; their coordination with each other also had to be determined. This engineering of the technical system was not done separately but alongside further elaboration of the architectural concept. This integrative and iterative design process (whose results were reported to Lloyd's in the outline proposal in June 1979, in the scheme design in June 1980 and finally in the detailed design in March 1982) allowed the design team to combine the two visionary ideas of the megastructure

65

and the intelligent environment in a holistic building design while considering the principle of legibility.

Services

RRP promised Lloyd's a building with low energy consumption already in the selection process. This goal was to be achieved by using well-known solutions such as high thermal insulation of the building envelope, heat recovery, and natural ventilation and lightning plus more novel ones like using night-time cooling to activate the thermal mass of the building or limiting the optimal building comfort to the workplace micro-climate – for all other areas in the building, an environment would be accepted between this optimum and the outside climate.[18] Especially this proposition for differentiated comfort zones reflected the idea of the intelligent environment, a basis for the new building from the outset.

Nevertheless, according to Tom Barker, the responsible building services engineer at Ove Arup, the environmental design of Lloyd's was originally based on a conventional system until RRP and Ove Arup & Partners discarded it at the end of 1979.[19] This conventional system would have used an air-to-water heat exchanger at the foot of the facade to heat and cool a zone of about 3.6 metres deep along the skin (4.10a–b), while the inner building area was to be cooled by ceiling-supplied air alone. Heated air was to be extracted at the ceiling and fed to a heat recovery system to optimise energy consumption. But this first system for air conditioning technology posed two main problems: first, the predicted energy demand at 0.9–1.0 gigajoules per square metre was 'unacceptably high'[20] – even considering the high number of workplaces. Second, the large air volume required to condition the Room would have resulted in a high density of ventilation ducts in the ceilings of each storey and on the outside of the building. For one thing, it was questionable whether commercially available air ducts along the facade could carry additional structural loads such as snow. But above all, the integration of the exhaust and supply air ducts in the floor and ceiling could not be solved satisfactorily, as shown in a sketch by Young (4.11a). In additional sketches, he examined various ideas like creating a duct-in-duct system, routing the exhaust air through the cavity of the raised floor or relocating the main lines of exhaust air into the interior of the atrium (4.11b–4.11g).

Since no solution could be found to solve these problems, Ove Arup & Partners started developing a new system for air conditioning with RRP in spring 1980, which was presented in a detailed report in September 1980 (4.12, 4.13).[21] The airflow was now floor to ceiling rather than ceiling to ceiling.[22] This meant that cooled supply air would be blown into the cavity of the raised floor, where it would be distributed unguided and mixed with room air that would be drawn in by local fans. The concrete slab below the cavity would act as a thermal sink. At night, the slab would be cooled by outside air to help keep the temperature low during the day. The air treated in the floor cavity would be fed back into the room via floor twist diffusers and nozzles integrated in the furniture. It would then rise along the heat sources – primarily people and machines – and collect two metres overhead in a heat reservoir that could rise to twenty-eight degrees Celsius. From there, the warm exhaust air would be drawn back via the ceiling lighting, led to the facade and blown into a cavity between the inner and outer glazing to the base point, from where it would finally reach the air plants via external ducts. To compensate for heat loads caused by solar radiation, local cooling units would be installed along the facade in the floor cavity. These units could also be operated in reverse to provide heating to the perimeter for warming the building in the morning.

A meeting note from Young, dated 20 May 1980, shows that this change of the air conditioning system took place relatively late in the design, just before the end of the scheme design phase (4.14a–b). The note mentions the name Krantz, a company which played a leading role in introducing floor supply systems with patented twist diffusers to the market.[23] One of the first office buildings to use this technology was the Klöckner building in Duisburg, Germany, completed in 1978.[24] A delegation from Lloyd's visited this building and the laboratories of the Krantz company in mid-September 1980 and was convinced of the effectiveness of this technology.[25]

The new air conditioning system resulted in a lower energy demand and ductwork that could be integrated within the storey ceiling because it solved many of the outstanding technical problems from the previous design. First, the mass of the floor slab could be activated as a thermal heat sink; second, the heat reservoir above head height reduced the cooling load; third, the exhaust air facade improved the comfort along the facade; and fourth, the density of installation could be greatly reduced. Additionally, the new air routing layout meant that the building would be further integrated with the air conditioning system: the floor and facade cavities, the furniture and the lighting would mutate into air-bearing elements (4.15, 4.16a–b).

Fusing the building with technology matched the ideas of megastructure and intelligent environment but generated new, unresolved questions of a technical and constructive nature that could not be clarified in the design stage. For the air conditioning system, the speed and temperature of

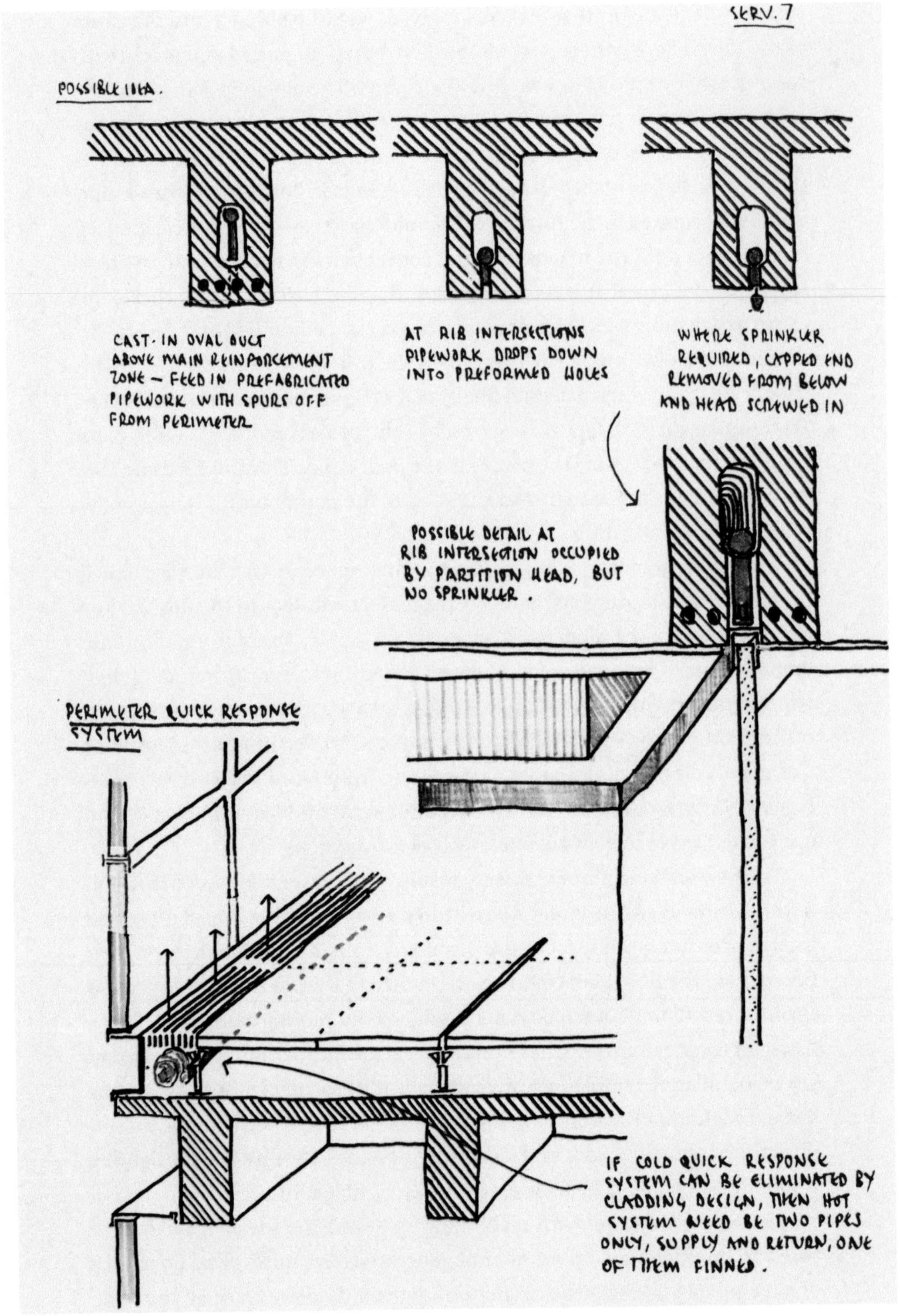

POSSIBLE IDEA.

CAST-IN OVAL DUCT
ABOVE MAIN REINFORCEMENT
ZONE — FEED IN PREFABRICATED
PIPEWORK WITH SPURS OFF
FROM PERIMETER.

AT RIB INTERSECTIONS
PIPEWORK DROPS DOWN
INTO PREFORMED HOLES

WHERE SPRINKLER
REQUIRED, CAPPED END
REMOVED FROM BELOW
AND HEAD SCREWED IN

POSSIBLE DETAIL AT
RIB INTERSECTION OCCUPIED
BY PARTITION HEAD, BUT
NO SPRINKLER.

PERIMETER QUICK RESPONSE
SYSTEM

IF COLD QUICK RESPONSE
SYSTEM CAN BE ELIMINATED BY
CLADDING DESIGN, THEN HOT
SYSTEM NEED BE TWO PIPES
ONLY, SUPPLY AND RETURN, ONE
OF THEM FINNED.

4.10a–b Design notes on the facade heating system, John Young, 23 September 1979

SERV. 8

IF ALL ELSE FAILS, AND WE MUST HAVE A PERIMETER
COLD RESPONSE ZONE, THEN EXTERNAL DUCT FEEDING INTO
UNDERFLOOR HEAT EXCHANGERS — INCREASES UNDERFLOOR ZONE AND CONSEQUENTLY
FLOOR TO FLOOR HEIGHT ENORMOUSLY.

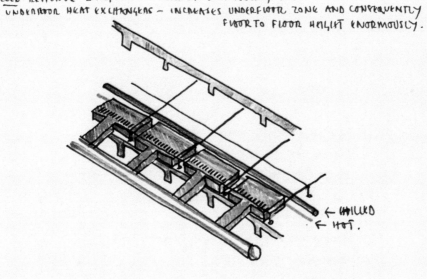

← CHILLED
← HOT.

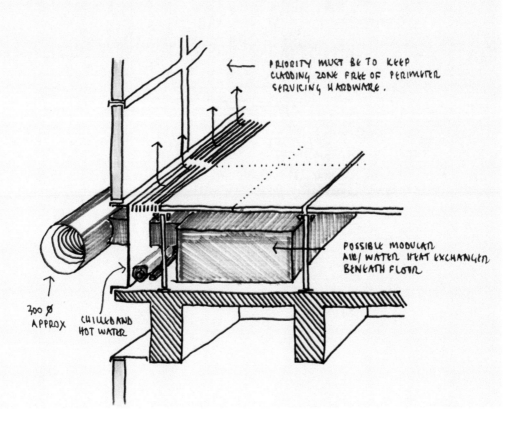

PRIORITY MUST BE TO KEEP
CLADDING ZONE FREE OF PERIMETER
SERVICING HARDWARE.

POSSIBLE MODULAR
AIR / WATER HEAT EXCHANGER
BENEATH FLOOR

300 Ø
APPROX

CHILLED AND
HOT WATER

69

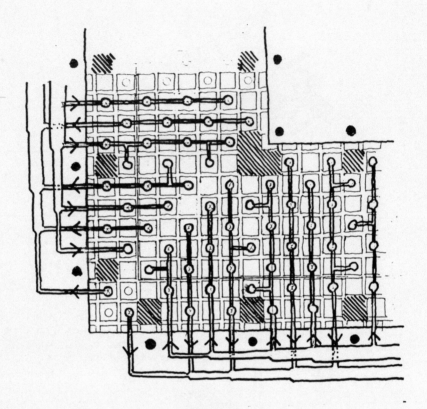

SKK V. 2

PLAN OF CORNER OF BUILDING
SHADING REPRESENTS STRUCTURAL ZONES.

J.Y. 1/9/79.

2 5

4.11a–b Design note on possible ways to integrate the ductwork in the floor slab, John Young,
1 September and 23 September 1979

SERV. 9

AIR DISTRIBUTION.

SUMMARY OF OAP DRAWINGS.

 SUPPLY

 EXTRACT

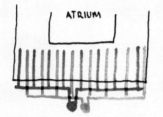

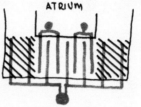

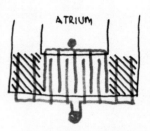

① 2·PIPE EXTERNAL SYSTEM

② EXTERNAL SUPPLY ATRIUM EXTRACT THRU' MANY VERTICALS. SHADED AREA NOT SERVED BY EXTRACT - THE CORNER PROBLEM

③ EXTERNAL SUPPLY. ATRIUM EXTRACT THRU' SINGLE DUCT - MORE IN KEEPING WITH HORIZONTAL DISTRIBUTION AND SINGLE VERTICAL RISER ON OUTSIDE FACE. CORNER PROBLEM STILL EXISTS.

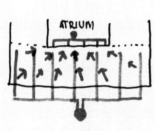

④ EXTERNAL SUPPLY, BUT EXTRACT PULLED THRU' A 10 CM RAISED FLOOR PLENUM TO OVERCOME CORNER PROBLEM. EXTRACT COLLECTED IN ONE VERTICAL DUCT IN ATRIUM.

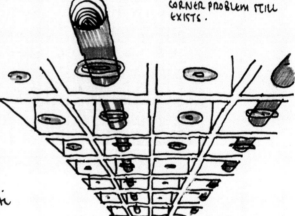

IF EXTRACT GOES THROUGH THE FLOOR, THEN 50% OF THE CEILING DUCTS DISAPPEAR - ONLY AT 3·6M CENTRES NOW.
SINCE LIGHTING IS INTEGRAL WITH A/C OUTLETS, A DIFFERENT LIGHT IS REQUIRED FOR NON-SUPPLY COFFERS WHERE NO DUCT EXIST. THERE ARE INSUFFICIENT COFFERS TO SUPPORT LIGHTING AND A/C OUTLETS IN SEPARATE ONES.

NOTE ROOM LIGHTING WILL NEED ADDITIONAL CAPABILITY TO DEAL WITH EXTRA FLOOR TO CEILING HEIGHT.

31

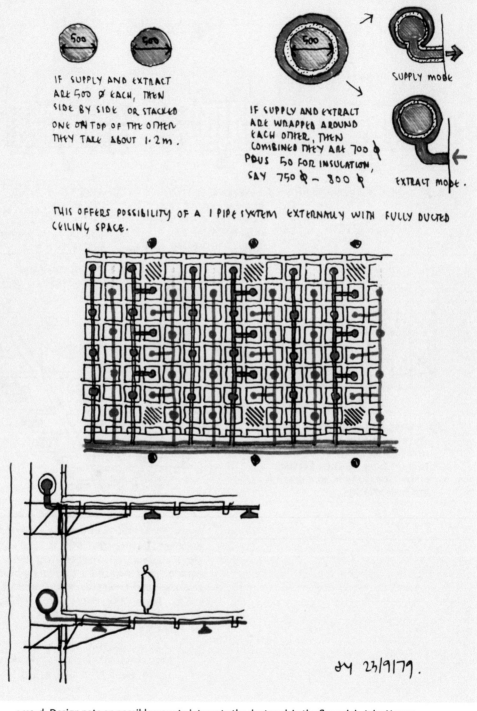

SERV. 10

IF SUPPLY AND EXTRACT
ARE 500 Ø EACH, THEN
SIDE BY SIDE OR STACKED
ONE ON TOP OF THE OTHER
THEY TAKE ABOUT 1·2m.

IF SUPPLY AND EXTRACT
ARE WRAPPED AROUND
EACH OTHER, THEN
COMBINED THEY ARE 700 Ø
PLUS 50 FOR INSULATION,
SAY 750 Ø ~ 800 Ø

SUPPLY MODE

EXTRACT MODE.

THIS OFFERS POSSIBILITY OF A 1 PIPE SYSTEM EXTERNALLY WITH FULLY DUCTED
CEILING SPACE.

JY 23/9/79.

4.11c–d Design note on possible ways to integrate the ductwork in the floor slab, John Young,
23 September and 10 October 1979

72

SERV. 11

LLOYD'S SERVICING

NOTES ON TOM BARKER / COLIN GRIFFITHS SESSION 1/10/79

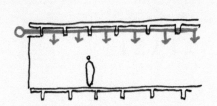

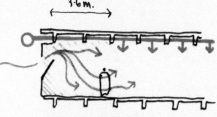

3·6 m.

NORMAL SITUATION
TREATED AIR DISCHARGED FROM ALL
TERMINALS IN SUPPLY DUCT

SUMMER CONDITION
OCCUPANT OPENS WINDOW, WHICH IS
CONNECTED ELECTRICALLY TO VALVE IN
PERIMETER ZONE TERMINALS, CLOSING
THEM OFF.

NOTE.
TO AVOID UNEVEN LIGHTING, EVERY COFFER
MUST HAVE A FITTING.

FURTHER THOUGHTS ON SERVICES DIRECTION

THE PROBLEM - ZONES.

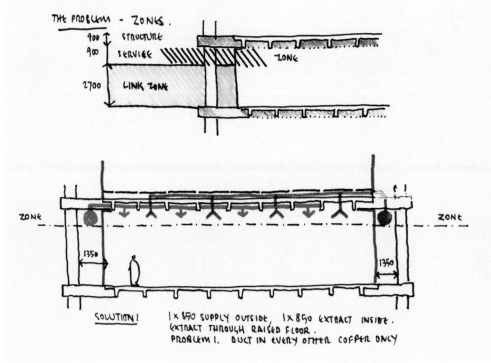

900 STRUCTURE
900 SERVICE ZONE
2700 LINK ZONE

ZONE

ZONE

ZONE

1350

1350

SOLUTION 1   1 x 850 SUPPLY OUTSIDE, 1 x 850 EXTRACT INSIDE.
EXTRACT THROUGH RAISED FLOOR.
PROBLEM 1. DUCT IN EVERY OTHER COFFER ONLY

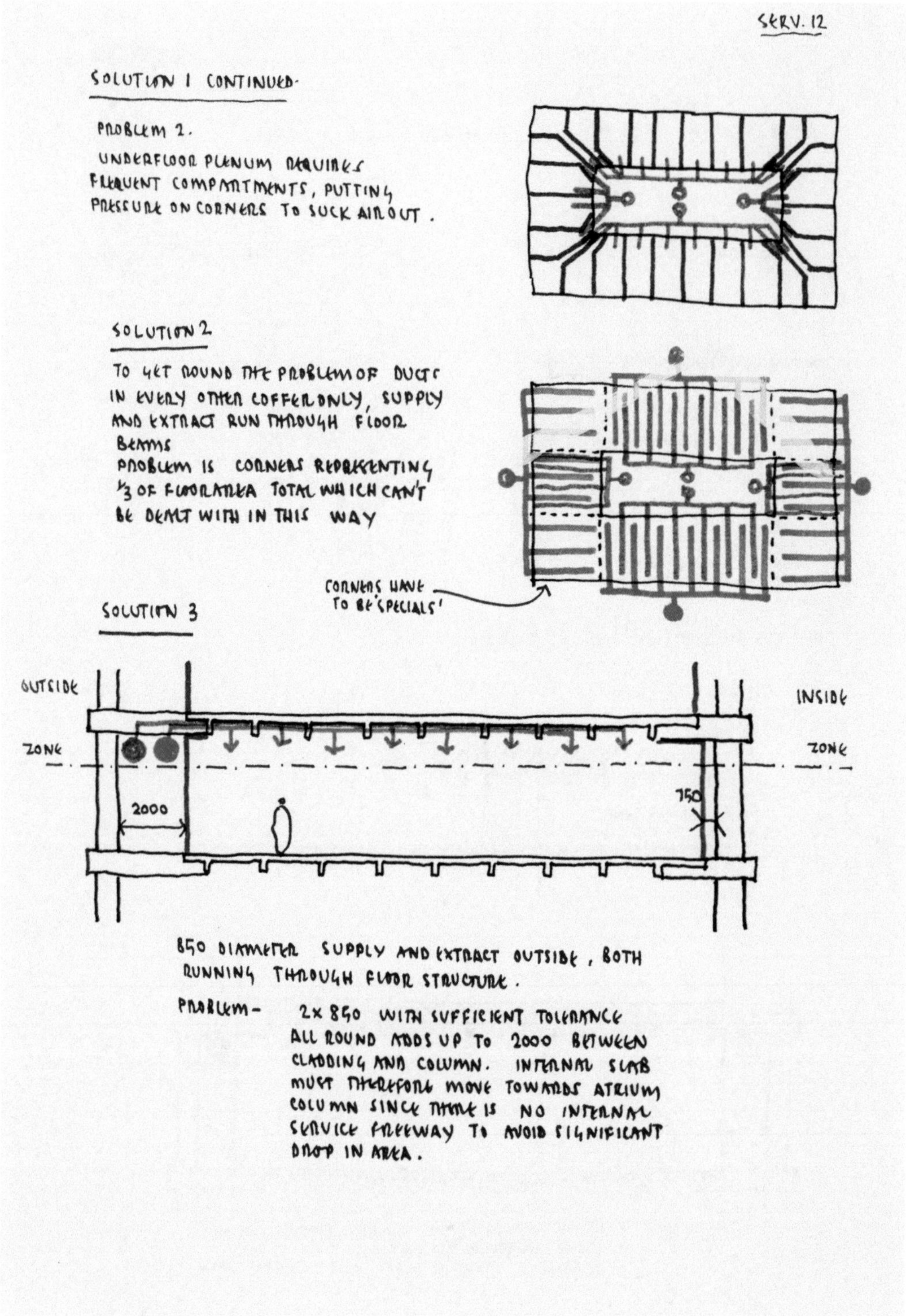

SOLUTION 1 CONTINUED.

PROBLEM 2.

UNDERFLOOR PLENUM REQUIRES
FREQUENT COMPARTMENTS, PUTTING
PRESSURE ON CORNERS TO SUCK AIR OUT.

SOLUTION 2

TO GET ROUND THE PROBLEM OF DUCTS
IN EVERY OTHER COFFER ONLY, SUPPLY
AND EXTRACT RUN THROUGH FLOOR
BEAMS
PROBLEM IS CORNERS REPRESENTING
⅓ OF FLOOR AREA TOTAL WHICH CAN'T
BE DEALT WITH IN THIS WAY

CORNERS HAVE
TO BE 'SPECIALS'

SOLUTION 3

OUTSIDE   INSIDE

ZONE   ZONE

2000   750

850 DIAMETER SUPPLY AND EXTRACT OUTSIDE, BOTH
RUNNING THROUGH FLOOR STRUCTURE.

PROBLEM —   2 × 850 WITH SUFFICIENT TOLERANCE
ALL ROUND ADDS UP TO 2000 BETWEEN
CLADDING AND COLUMN. INTERNAL SLAB
MUST THEREFORE MOVE TOWARDS ATRIUM
COLUMN SINCE THERE IS NO INTERNAL
SERVICE FREEWAY TO AVOID SIGNIFICANT
DROP IN AREA.

4.11e–f Design note on possible ways to integrate the ductwork in the floor slab, John Young,
10 October 1979

UP TILL NOW THE SERVICES
DIAGRAM HAS BEEN, SERVICE
SATELLITES NOS 2, 3, 5 AND
6. LONGEST RUNS IN NOS. 1
AND 3 DETERMINE MAXIMUM
SIZE DUCT AT 850 mm ⌀

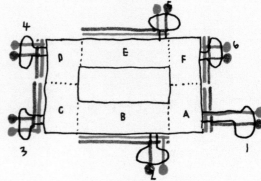

SOLUTION 4

IF ALL SIX SATELLITES
BECOME SERVICES, THEN
2 AND 5 BECOME THE
LONGEST RUNS AND ON A
PRO RATA BASIS, THEN THE
MAXIMUM DUCT SIZE SHOULD
BE ABLE TO REDUCE TO 600 mm ⌀
COLIN GRIFFITHS TO VERIFY.

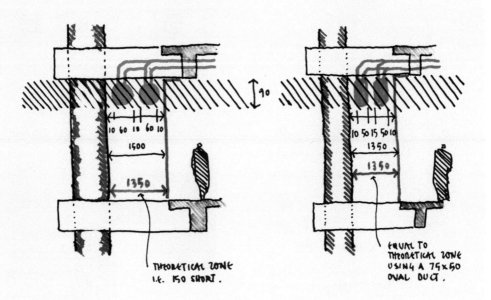

THEORETICAL ZONE
I.E. 150 SHORT.

EQUAL TO
THEORETICAL ZONE
USING A 75×50
OVAL DUCT.

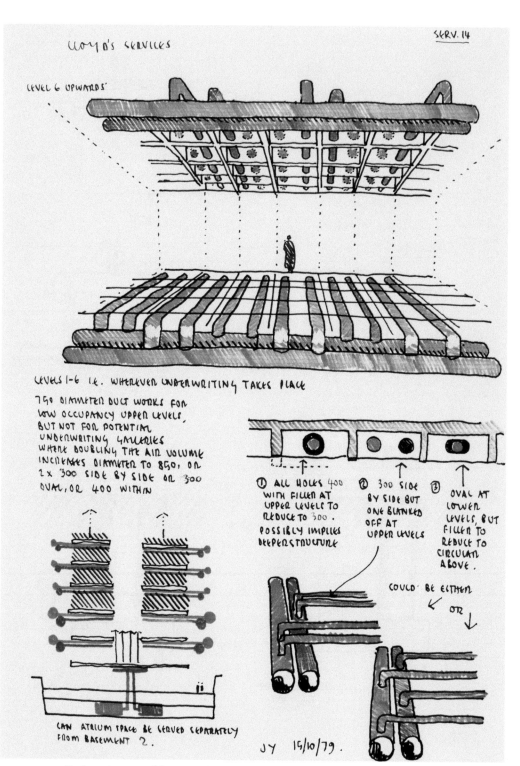

4.11g Design note on possible ways to integrate the ductwork in the floor slab, John Young,
15 October 1979

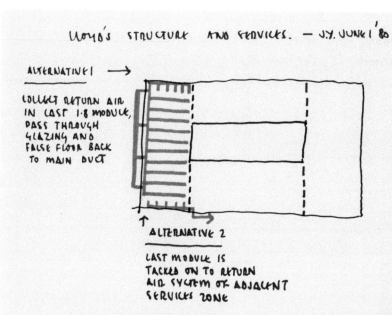

SERV. 15

LLOYD'S STRUCTURE AND SERVICES. — J.Y. JUNE '80

ALTERNATIVE I →

COLLECT RETURN AIR
IN LAST 1.8 MODULE,
PASS THROUGH
GLAZING AND
FALSE FLOOR BACK
TO MAIN DUCT

ALTERNATIVE 2

LAST MODULE IS
TACKED ON TO RETURN
AIR SYSTEM OF ADJACENT
SERVICES ZONE

EITHER WAY, EXTENT OF SERVICES COVER TO FACADE VIRTUALLY EQUAL
CURRENT MODEL — FOR NEATNESS THEREFORE, ALTERNATIVE I IS
PREFERABLE.

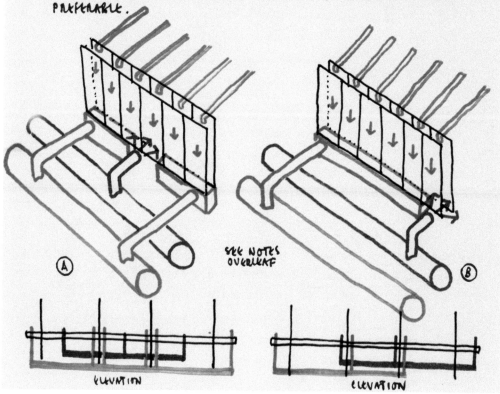

Ⓐ SEE NOTES OVERLEAF Ⓑ

ELEVATION   ELEVATION

4.12 Design notes on new air conditioning system with exhaust air facade, John Young,
1 June 1980

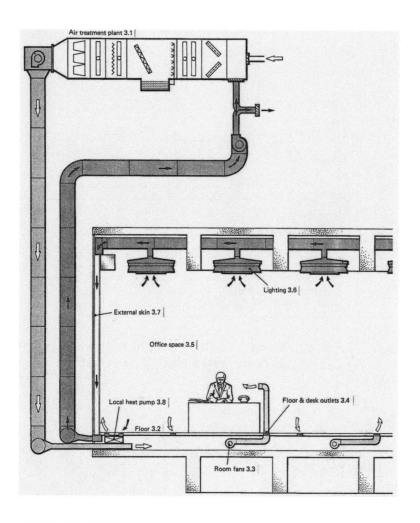

Air treatment plant 3.1

Lighting 3.6

External skin 3.7

Office space 3.5

Local heat pump 3.8

Floor 3.2

Floor & desk outlets 3.4

Room fans 3.3

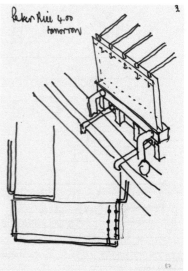

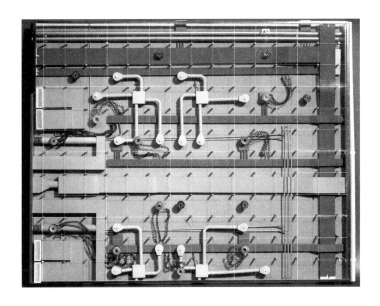

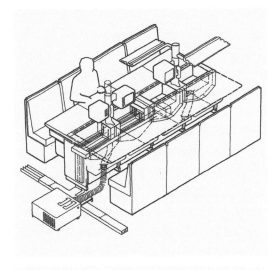

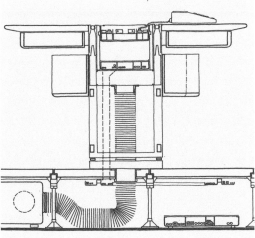

4.13 Diagram of new air conditioning system, Ove Arup & Partners,
September 1980

4.14a–b Meeting notes the new air
conditioning system, John Young,
20 May 1980

4.15 Model of cable routing in
raised floor

4.16 Early version of the underwriter box: the supply air is guided
via a profile system to the desktop,
where it is blown into the room
by nozzles

a Axonometric
b Cross section

the airflows supplying the room and within the facade cavity would have to be specified to ensure that the system could compensate for heat and cold. Additionally, tests would have to be carried out with both the new floor twist diffusers and the nozzles for the boxes to ensure that the required air quality and comfort could be achieved. Furthermore, ceiling lights with integrated exhaust air and sprinkler heads would have to be developed and the load limits of the external ventilation ducts tested.

Structure

For the design of the structural system, RRP collaborated with Rice and various engineers from Ove Arup & Partners.[25] As Rice pointed out, the search for a suitable ceiling structure was the starting point for the entire structural system: 'The structure has been developed from the problem of the Ring floor.'[27] The conditions for this Ring floor formed by the void of the atrium were derived directly from the typology of the atrium tower and the concept of a homogeneous adaptable space. The floor slab was designed to carry a relatively heavy load at four kilonewtons per square metre (eighty pounds per square foot) to account for the high density of people on the floor and to allow for flexibility in future use.[28] To be able to use this space as efficiently as possible and to make the supporting structure legible from the outside, the required ceiling construction had to span the entire depth of the room so that columns and horizontal bracing could be positioned outside the building envelope. In accordance with the spatial concept, the ceiling structure needed to emphasize the unity of the space and be read as a section of a continuum. In addition, all cables, ducts and technical equipment were to be integrated into the ceiling construction to be freely accessible for adjustments in the event of future changes in usage.

As a sketch from Ove Arup & Partners of the spatial coordination of the various elements of the ceiling structure and the building services shows (4.17a–b), the conditions for the ceiling structure led to two opposing requirements, namely a high static load-bearing capacity and high permeability for the horizontal duct and cable routing. In the search for a suitable solution Ove Arup & Partners was inspired by the work of Louis Kahn, whose Yale University Art Gallery was a particularly important source in the design process.[29] As various sketches by Ove Arup & Partners show, a number of other ceiling structures, from isometric support panels to vaulted ceilings, were also examined (4.18a–c).

Ultimately, the decision for an orthogonal beam grid[30] was the most obvious choice from both an architectural and a structural point of view. In

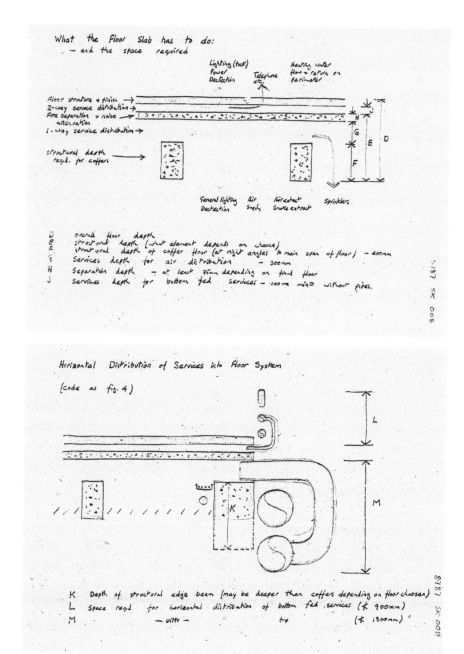

The figure contains the following handwritten annotations:

What the Floor Slab has to do:
— and the space required

Lighting (task)
Power
Detection
Telephone etc.
Heating water flow + return on perimeter

Floor structure + finish →
2-way service distribution →
Fire separation + noise attenuation →
1-way service distribution →

structural depth reqd. for coffers →

General lighting
Detection
Air supply
Air extract
Smoke extract
Sprinklers

D overall floor depth
E structural depth (what element depends on choice)
G structural depth of coffer floor (at right angles to main span of floor) — 400mm
I Services depth for air distribution — 300mm
H Separation depth — at least 75mm depending on final floor
J Services depth for bottom fed services — 100mm min? without pipes.

SK 008   V187

Horizontal Distribution of Services into Floor System

(code as fig. 4)

K Depth of structural edge beam (may be deeper than coffers depending on floor chosen)
L Space reqd. for horizontal distribution of bottom fed services (≮ 900mm)
M — ditto —   (≮ 1300mm)

SK 009   V187

4.17a–b 'What the floor slab has to do – and the space required', Ove Arup & Partners

contrast to a unidirectional structure, which would have divided the ceiling into two parallel fields on its long sides and fillers on its short sides, the bidirectional orthogonal beam grid on the underside of the ceiling slab would appear as a homogeneous, continuous grid from which the void of the atrium was omitted. The appearance of the ceiling in the ring-shaped room, whether a corner segment or longitudinal section, would thus always be the same. Moreover, from the point of view of statics, the beam grid

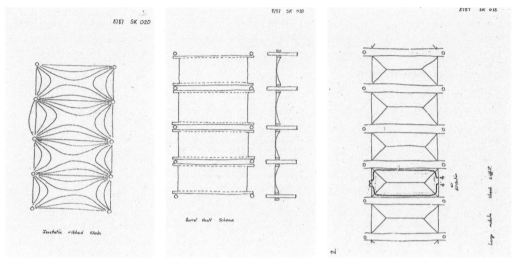

4.18 Sketches of possible structural systems for the floor slab, Ove Arup & Partners
a Isostatic ribs
b Barrel vaulting
c Sloping soffit

embodied the ideal of an infinitely redundant system. Due to the many different paths across which force could be transmitted, the loads would be distributed horizontally across the beams. This system thus enabled wide-span structures because the grid could pick up loads at any point and transfer them vertically to the ground.

Outlining the structural system

After the decision to construct the ceiling as a beam grid, the focus of the structural design could be expanded to all elements of the structural system, especially to the ceiling and column supports. When placing them along the building, the spacing of the 1.8-metre beam grid and the dimensions of the atrium and the building body had to be considered. Because the main building had to be optimally fitted between the satellite towers on the tightly dimensioned plot, both dimensions changed several times during the design due to the increased size of the servant elements in the towers. Since the position of the columns defined the support points of the beam grid, each of these changes had a direct effect on the distribution of the forces over the different beams and ultimately on their dimensioning.

Ove Arup & Partners and RRP solved the interdependent questions concerning the column placing, the dimensioning of the beam grid, the design of the slab support and the horizontal bracing of the structural framework in a lengthy, iterative process that lasted from the outline proposal phase to the detailed design phase. A comparison of different stages of the project shows that RRP successively reduced the number of columns and shifted its position in response to the changes in the dimensions of the main building and the atrium (4.19a–4.19f).

The first structural framework of the outline proposal, presented to the redevelopment committee in June 1979, exploited the static potential of an orthogonal beam grid to distribute forces in two directions. The offset arrangement of the columns along the facade and in the atrium would ensure that the main load-bearing directions in the beam grid run diagonally to the two sets of beams (4.19b). The flow of forces would thus be distributed more evenly over the beams and subject each to similar loads.[31] In the recessed upper floors, however, this configuration with offset columns would lead to unmanageable overhangs and spans (4.20). While the beam grid was designed as a concrete structure, the columns were designed as stainless steel tubes filled with water. In the event of fire, an elaborate circuit with separate pipes for the inflow and outflow of cooling water would keep the steel temperature of the columns within the permissible range of the increased fire protection requirements.

Pairing the columns

In mid-1979, the arrangement of the columns was altered[32] to solve the conceptual problems of the structural design in the recessed upper floors by inserting a column on each of the outer sides of the building and placing the outer and inner columns on the same axis (4.19c). Pairing the columns solved the problem of overhangs and spans in the recessed floors and created a visual regularity in the interior, but it negatively affected the statics of the beam grid: positioning pairs of inner and outer columns on the axes of the beam grid introduced a primary flow of force on these column lines, creating a hierarchy of the beams. The loads that flowed into these beams were too much to be able to be handled with the available height.[33] Not only would load-bearing capacity need to be improved, the deformation of the beam grid from deflection also had to be minimised to prevent cracks in the exposed concrete and guarantee the tolerance range of the structure. The permissible deviations were a challenge for the construction industry in Great Britain at the time, but meeting this challenge was necessary to ensure the smooth assembly of prefabricated facade elements that were also planned for the Lloyd's Building (4.21).[34]

To overcome the static deficiencies that resulted from the new column configuration, Ove Arup & Partners pursued two strategies. First, the team

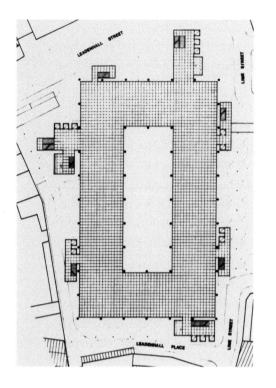

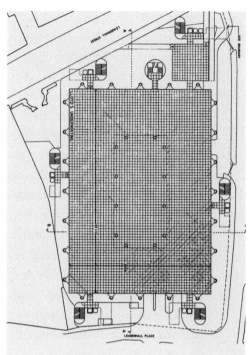

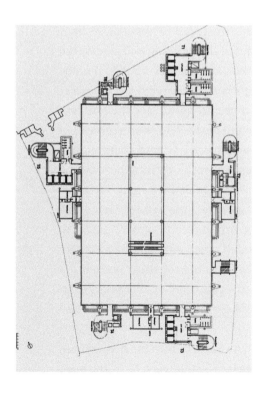

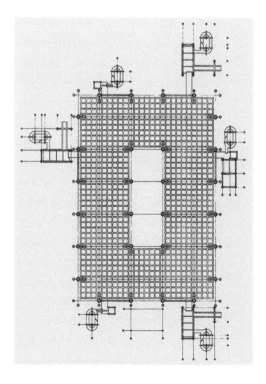

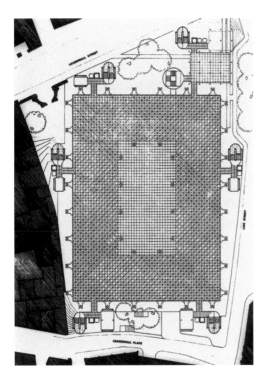 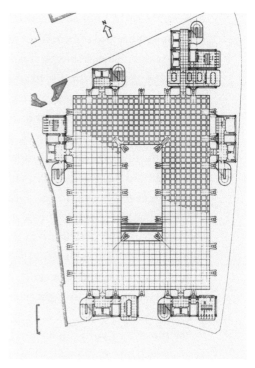

4.19 Evolution of the main building structure

a Development strategy, October 1978
b Outline proposal, April 1979: columns along the facade are shifted in relation to columns in the atrium
c Reworked outline proposal, June 1979: the number of external columns is increased to align them with the columns in the atrium
d Reworked outline proposal, October 1979: 9 × 9 m column grid
e Scheme design, June 1980: 10.8 × 10.8 m column grid
f Detailed design, March 1982

explored ways to improve the stiffness of the beam grid, but these reduced its permeability and thus made it more difficult to integrate the ductwork in the floor slab. Next, it tried to improve the moment line of the beam by reducing the span, but this led to complex ceiling supports. Young's sketches from October 1979 show different variations for brackets that shifted the support point from the column into the interior of the building (4.22a–d), reducing the span of the beam by two grid modules (from 18 to 14.4 metres). At the same time, the brackets together with the columns and the beam grid formed a rigid frame that could absorb the horizontal forces.[35]

Further sketches by Young show considerations of how the production of the beam grid could be solved with prefabricated parts (4.23a–b). Yet for the forces to freely distribute in the beam grid, all of the beams had to be rigidly connected to each other. While this would be the case with monolithic, in-situ concrete constructions, it is difficult to achieve with precast elements. Therefore, these thoughts were not pursued further as they would have been too costly.

By the end of 1979 the design team had heavily revised the structure.[36] The external dimensions of the building and the void of the atrium had been significantly reduced to make room for the enlarged satellite towers. The number of columns on the outside of the building again corresponded to the outline proposal status of early 1979. The position of the inner columns, however, was changed. The inner corner of the atrium was no longer free, occupied now by a column on which a bracket reached diagonally far into the beam grid. The remaining ceiling supports were placed far away from the columns to reduce the span (4.19d).

Considering a tie-down system

In the scheme design presented in June 1980, the number of columns was reduced even further so that the facade and atrium columns lay on a regular grid (4.19e, 4.24). The fields of the beam grid measured 10.8 by 16.2 metres at the sides and 16.2 by 16.2 metres at the corners of the building. While the beam grid at the inner columns was supported by brackets, at the outer columns it was connected to a tie-down system (4.25a–b): two beams from the grid were extended past each column to which they were attached, and tied to the ground by rods. The tie-down system introduced a negative moment at the end of the beam, thus reducing the main moment at the centre of the

4.20 Outline proposal: building axonometry, 1979. Large overhangs and spans in the recessed floors occurred due to the staggered configuration of the columns.

86

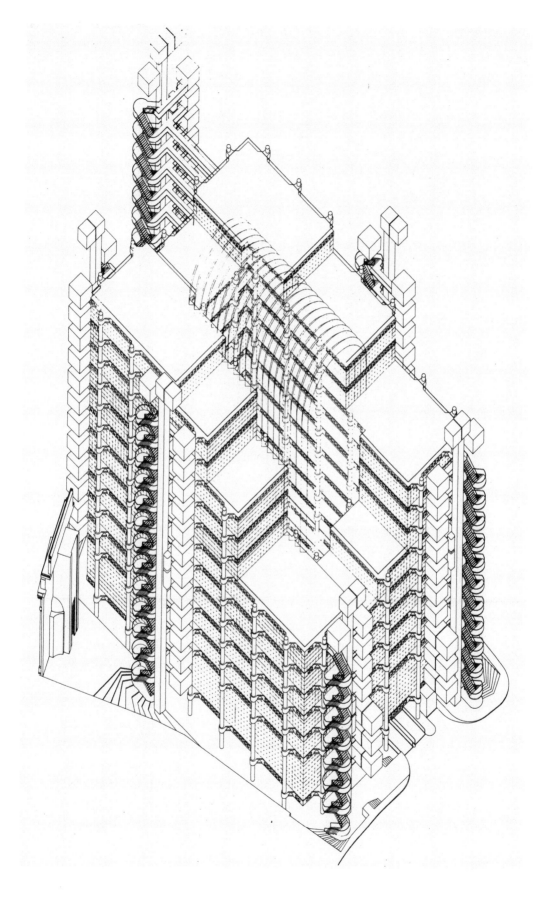

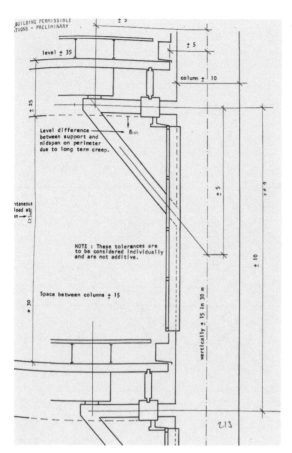

4.21 Permissible deviations,
Stephen Le Roith, October 1980

beam so that the beam at the available height could bear the load. However, the new support of the floor slab with a tie-down system could no longer be activated as bracing against horizontal forces. Instead, this function would now be performed by diagonal bracing between two columns. Since the installations to cool the columns with water in case of fire were too expensive, the columns were now designed to be filled with concrete. To reduce the load on the support, the columns would be placed directly on the facade and the horizontal ventilation ducts run between the columns and the tie-downs. The distance between column and tie-downs thus became the determining factor for the ducting along the facade (4.25e).

Even if this new structure fulfilled its load-bearing purpose, it would produce various problems. Not only did the ceiling support penetrate the facade and create complex connection details, it also protruded into the interior, obstructing the passage area along the inner facade (4.25a, 4.25d). The tie-downs of the individual floors had to be bundled together in steel-clad concrete pipes with a diameter so large that they would be legible as small columns instead as tie-downs. Finally, the structure of the beam grid was still not isotropic. The high installation density meant that the beams parallel to the facade would have to be shaped at half height, which on the one hand would impair the load-bearing behaviour of the structure, especially in the corner sections, and on the other hand would require a laborious formwork (4.25c).[37]

Pre-stressing the beam grid

Only during the detailed design phase was a solution finally found that met all the requirements for the structure. According to Rice, the key to this was understanding the flow of forces within the beam grid: 'The solution to this problem came by observing the natural flow of forces in the grid, in particular the attraction to the column line.'[38] This flow of forces is not trivial, since the static system of a beam grid is multiply indeterminate and, prior to the development of computer-aided methods, could only be calculated with great effort.

Although Ove Arup & Partners had computers, the team preferred doing calculations manually in the early stages of the project. This forced engineers to study the mechanics of the system more intensively and usually led to a better understanding of the structure.[39] Manual calculations were also often faster at that time because computer access was limited due to the slow speeed and scarcity of mainframe computers on which such calculations could be processed. Computational methods were typically used only to validate and specify the conclusions drawn from the manual calculations. Since the flow of forces in the Lloyd's Building could no longer be reproduced on paper, however, a corner field of 16.8 by 16.8 metres finally had to be analysed with the help of the computer.[40] The calculations showed that the natural flow of forces would place the greatest stress on the beam on the column axes, thus confirming the estimate from the manual calculations.

The engineers addressed these findings directly by strengthening and stiffening the two beams on the column lines: they were joined with a slab on top to form an inverted U-profile and prestressed. This measure acted as a relief for the entire structural design. By using prestressed U-beams, all sections (including the corner sections of 16.8 by 16.8 metres) could be spanned with beam grids of half-height beams of fifty-five by thirty centimetres. The deformation under load still posed a problem in the corner sections but could be solved by pre-stressing these beams in addition to the U-beams. Above the beam grid, a 13.5-centimetre thick concrete slab, poured into a sound-absorbing permanent formwork made of steel panels,

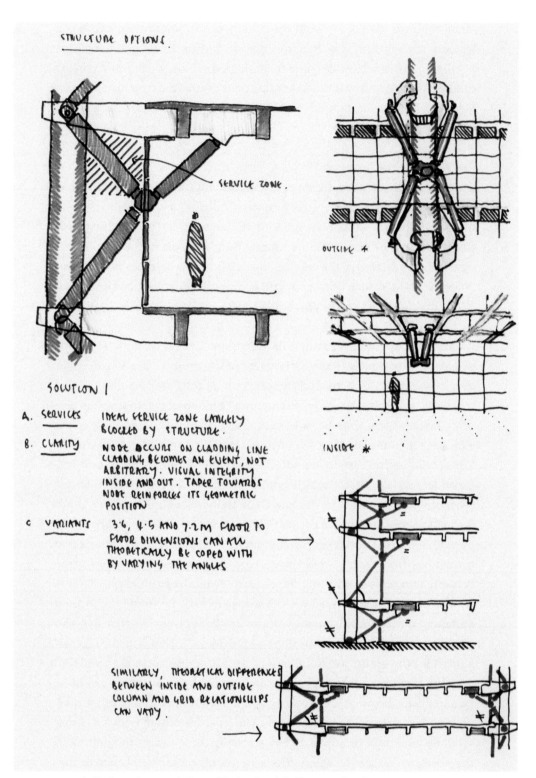

STRUCTURE OPTIONS

SERVICE ZONE.

OUTSIDE ✦

INSIDE ✱

SOLUTION 1

A. SERVICES — IDEAL SERVICE ZONE LARGELY BLOCKED BY STRUCTURE.

B. CLARITY — NODE OCCURS ON CLADDING LINE CLADDING BECOMES AN EVENT, NOT ARBITRARY. VISUAL INTEGRITY INSIDE AND OUT. TAPER TOWARDS NODE REINFORCES ITS GEOMETRIC POSITION

C. VARIANTS — 3·6, 4·5 AND 7·2M FLOOR TO FLOOR DIMENSIONS CAN ALL THEORETICALLY BE COPED WITH BY VARYING THE ANGLES →

SIMILARLY, THEORETICAL DIFFERENCES BETWEEN INSIDE AND OUTSIDE COLUMN AND GRID RELATIONSHIPS CAN VARY. →

4.22a–b Design notes on variations of the bracket, John Young, 30 October 1979

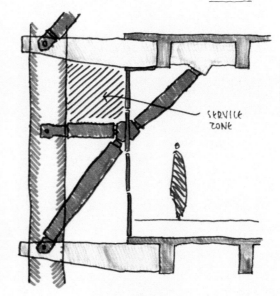

STRUCT. 7.

SERVICE ZONE

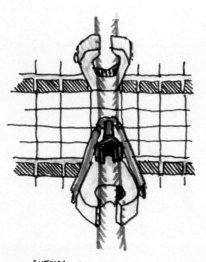

OUTSIDE *

SOLUTION 2.

A. SERVICES   OPTIMUM SERVICE ZONE
B. CLARITY   INHERENT BLINDNESS.
ALTHOUGH NODE OCCURS ON
CLADDING LINE AS BEFORE, ABSENCE
OF UPPER DIAGONAL STRUT GIVES
IMPRESSION THAT BRACKET SUPPORTS
GLAZING, OR MORE ACCURATELY,
THAT BRACKET IS 'SUSPENDED'
FROM CLADDING — UNSATISFACTORY.

C. VARIANTS THEORETICALLY AS SOLUTION 1.

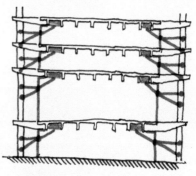

• • • • ● ● • • •

SOLUTION 3.

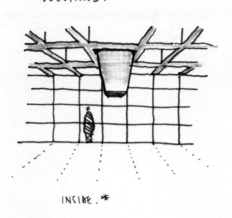

INSIDE. *

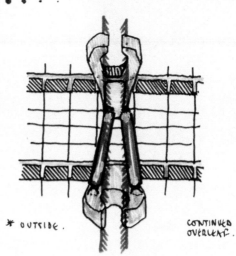

* OUTSIDE.

CONTINUED OVERLEAF.

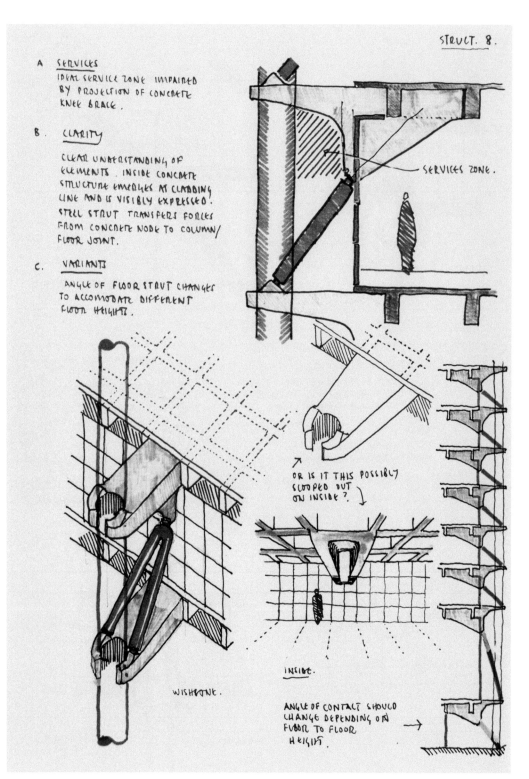

STRUCT. 8.

A SERVICES
IDEAL SERVICE ZONE IMPAIRED
BY PROJECTION OF CONCRETE
KNEE BRACE.

B. CLARITY

CLEAR UNDERSTANDING OF
ELEMENTS. INSIDE CONCRETE
STRUCTURE EMERGES AT CLADDING
LINE AND IS VISIBLY EXPRESSED.
STEEL STRUT TRANSFERS FORCES
FROM CONCRETE NODE TO COLUMN/
FLOOR JOINT.

C. VARIANTS

ANGLE OF FLOOR STRUT CHANGES
TO ACCOMODATE DIFFERENT
FLOOR HEIGHTS.

— SERVICES ZONE.

↗ OR IS IT THIS POSSIBLY
SCOOPED OUT
ON INSIDE? ↓

WISHBONE.

INSIDE.

ANGLE OF CONTACT SHOULD
CHANGE DEPENDING ON
FLOOR TO FLOOR
HEIGHT. →

4.22c–d Design notes on variations of the bracket, John Young, 30 October 1979

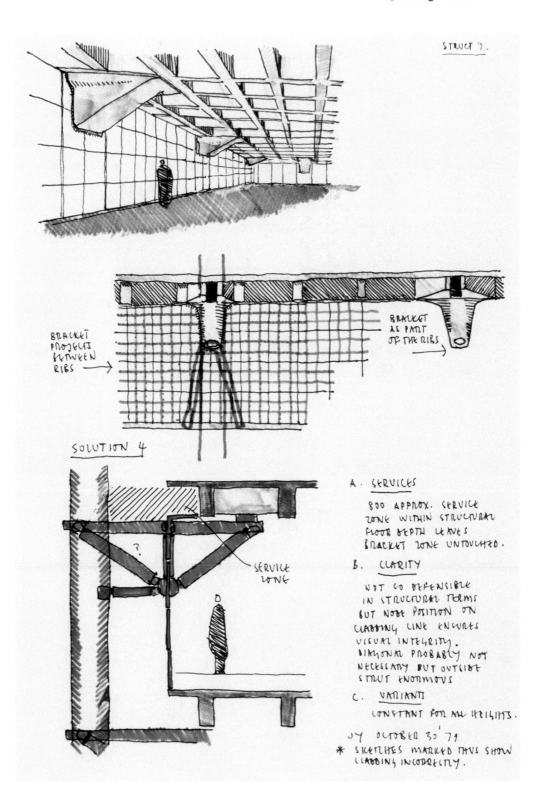

STRUCT 9.

BRACKET
PROJECTS
BETWEEN
RIBS →

← BRACKET
AS PART
OF THE RIBS

SOLUTION 4

SERVICE
ZONE

A. SERVICES

800 APPROX. SERVICE
ZONE WITHIN STRUCTURAL
FLOOR DEPTH LEAVES
BRACKET ZONE UNTOUCHED.

B. CLARITY

NOT SO DEFENSIBLE
IN STRUCTURAL TERMS
BUT NOTE POSITION ON
CLADDING LINE ENSURES
VISUAL INTEGRITY.
DIAGONAL PROBABLY NOT
NECESSARY BUT OUTSIDE
STRUT ENORMOUS

C. VARIANTS

CONSTANT FOR ALL HEIGHTS.

JY OCTOBER 30' 79

* SKETCHES MARKED THUS SHOW
CLADDING INCORRECTLY.

93

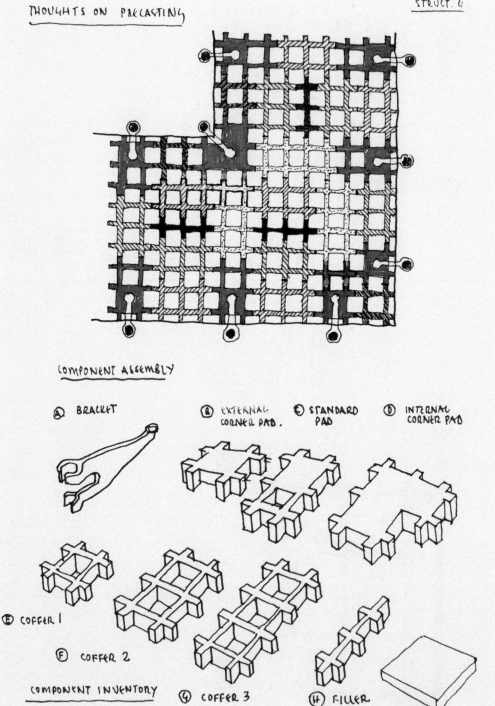

THOUGHTS ON PRECASTING

STRUCT. 4

COMPONENT ASSEMBLY

(A) BRACKET

(B) EXTERNAL CORNER PAD.

(C) STANDARD PAD

(D) INTERNAL CORNER PAD

(E) COFFER 1

(F) COFFER 2

COMPONENT INVENTORY

(G) COFFER 3

(H) FILLER

(J) SLAB.

4.23a–b Design notes on the beam grid with assembled, prefabricated elements, John Young, 30 October 1979

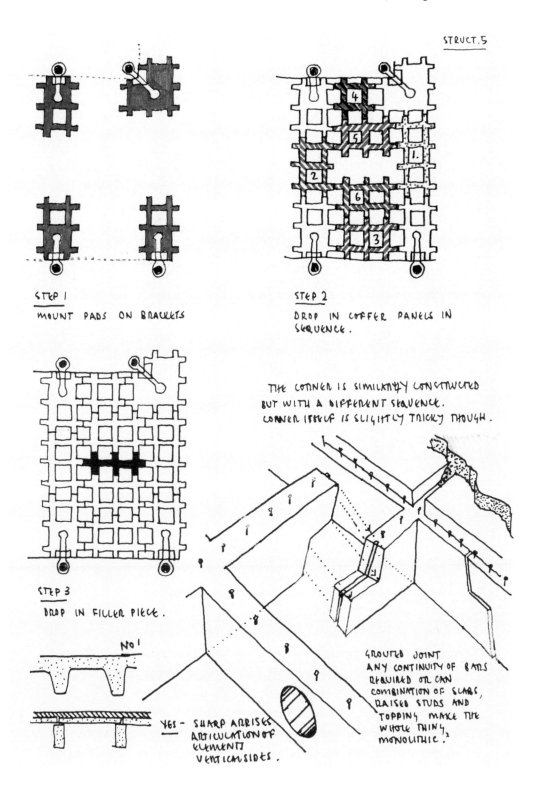

STRUCT.5

STEP 1
MOUNT PADS ON BRACKETS

STEP 2
DROP IN COFFER PANELS IN SEQUENCE.

STEP 3
DROP IN FILLER PIECE.

NO!

YES - SHARP ARRISES
ARTICULATION OF
ELEMENTS
VERTICAL SIDES.

THE CORNER IS SIMILARLY CONSTRUCTED
BUT WITH A DIFFERENT SEQUENCE.
CORNER ITSELF IS SLIGHTLY TRICKY THOUGH.

GROUTED JOINT
ANY CONTINUITY OF BARS
REQUIRED OR CAN
COMBINATION OF SLABS,
RAISED STUDS AND
TOPPING MAKE THE
WHOLE THING
MONOLITHIC.

95

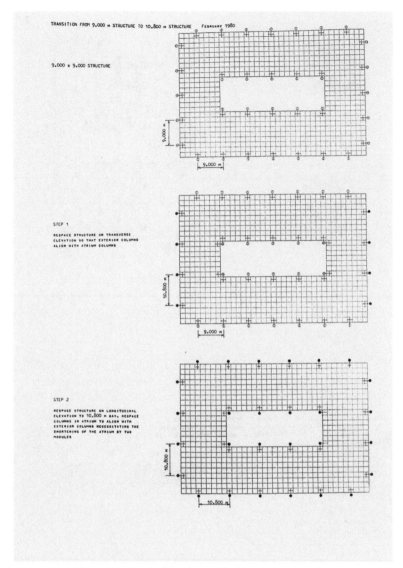

4.24 Notes on the consequences of the changed building grid, February 1980

would rest on stub columns (the remaining part of the original girder) 46.5 centimetres high to separate the individual floors from each other and create a generous space for the ductwork. Service penetrations in the U-beams would only be necessary in individual cases (4.26a–c).

The brackets for the beam grid support could also be simplified: since the support no longer would have to cantilever so far, it could be significantly shorter and therefore fit inside the beam grid without penetrating the glazing. Although the forces in the bracket would still have to be conducted using steel parts, these could now be encased in concrete for fire protection. On the console's sides, the horizontal bracings could be fixed. These would consist of steel tubes encased in concrete to increase fire resistance (4.27, 4.28).

Finally, the steel casing of the columns was also relinquished so that the entire structure appeared to be made of concrete. The columns were manufactured in situ, with the bracket covering the construction joint between the floors like a sleeve (4.29). The column, bracket and bracing joint was articulated in a node, making the principle of the structure legible from the outside. In its first (and probably only) monthly progress report, from 16 June 1981, Ove Arup & Partners reported, 'Floor structure fully schemed – ready for final design. Brackets and bearings fully schemed – ready for final design, after RRP approval of shapes. Column ready for final design.' [41] According to Rice, the structural solution originated from a moment of inspiration:

> The complete structural solution for the floor of the Lloyd's of London building came to my mind one evening in Turin while I was working on the Fiat project. ... We had been discussing the problem very thoroughly during the previous weeks, so it is not surprising that I should have been thinking of a possible solution. But that the solution should arise fully formed is, I think, unusual. It is characteristic of the way engineers think: because they are working with objective parameters these lead to only one conclusion. [42]

Although the structural elements were dimensioned and their shape determined, there were still several technical issues that had to be clarified before assembling column, bracket, bracing and grid and before producing the beam grid. As in any monolithic concrete structure the appearance of the beam grid was determined by its formwork. Although concrete is poured, its formwork counterpart is constructed. The formwork's joining would be visible in the monolithic concrete, so its assembly would be legible. The common construction method with tapered fibreglass moulds was not an option: the appearance was associated with multi-storey car parks where this method was used commonly and therefore seemed unsuitable for the high standards of Lloyd's. Instead, RRP decided that the beam grid should have parallel flanks, sharp edges and a smooth finish. Yet how to join the sequence of the brackets and columns remained unresolved. Before starting construction, technical questions had to be clarified concerning the surface quality of the visible in-situ concrete, the production process and the formwork system for the beam grid and the U-beam, the lost formwork for the floor slab and the assembly of brackets and columns.

4.25 Scheme design with tie-down
system
a Model of a typical storey
b Model of the facade

c Floor plan showing beam grid
with different beam heights,
June 1980
d Detailed facade section showing
penetration of glazing by bracket,
June 1980
e Clearance for ductwork, RRP,
December 1979

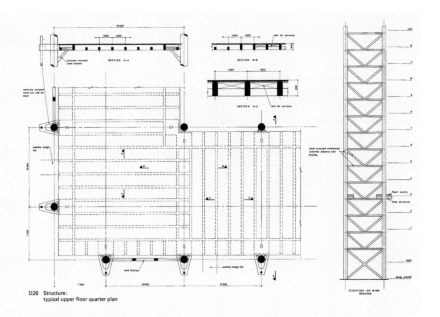

D26 Structure:
typical upper floor quarter plan

ELEVATION ON WIND BRACING

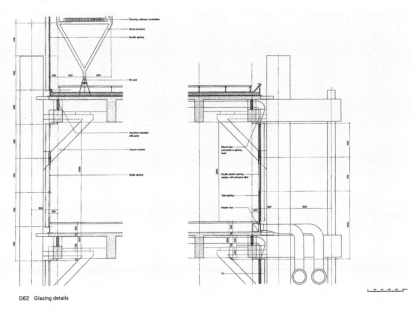

D62 Glazing details

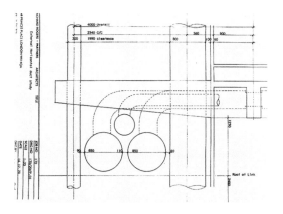

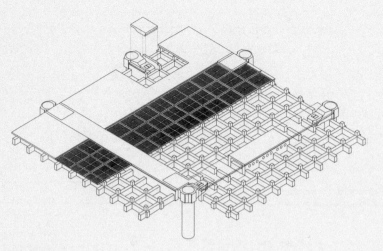

400/226 Main frame
Cutaway isometric

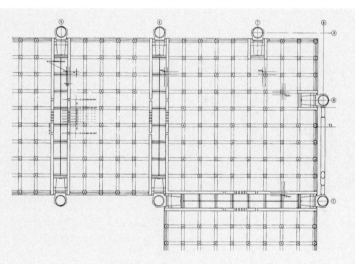

5

400/374 Main frame
Typical gallery condition: Reflected plan concrete soffit

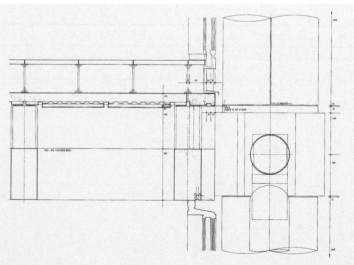

15

400/334 Main frame
Section at mid-span of braced bay: Edge condition of floor slab

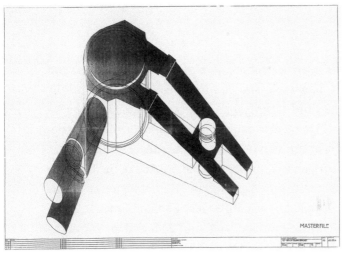

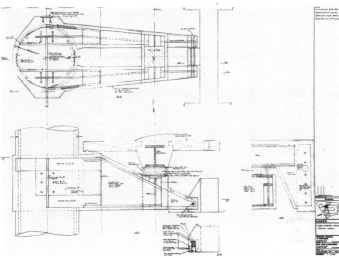

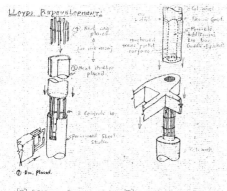

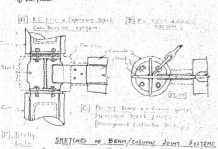

4.26 Detailed design: main structure, March 1982

a Cutaway isometric illustrating construction of the floor
b Plan of the beam grid
c Detailed facade section

4.27 Column bracket bracing assembly, RRP, May 1981

4.28 Column bracket assembly showing steel-work and concrete casing, Ove Arup & Partners, June 1981

4.29 Variations on the column bracket assembly, September 1980

Envelope

In addition to the building service technologies and the structure, the concept of a homogeneous, adaptable and comfortable space relied on the building envelope as the third technical system. As a boundary layer between the controlled intelligent environment and the uncontrolled exterior environment, the envelope, comparable to a membrane, controls the passage of radiation and heat between the inside and outside of the building. Its properties thus influence natural lighting, the thermal comfort of the building's interior and ultimately the qualities of the spatial concept. To fulfil these qualities, the building envelope could not be based on any of the products available on the market and would have to be developed from scratch. Unlike the building service technology and engineered structure from Ove Arup & Partners, RRP would design the envelope and the supporting structure without specialist engineers, so the team cooperated with the building industry from very early on.

During the early stage of the design, in contrast to the building services and the structure, hardly any design was done on the building envelope. RRP concentrated its work on the search for a material that would both prevent people from looking in from outside (thus providing a protected setting for business and negotiations) and provide the deep rooms of the building with optimal daylight. The glass block facade of the Maison de Verre (4.30) by Pierre Chareau was an important reference for the desired quality of light in the interior:

> We enjoy this [the way the facade is constructed] because of its three-dimensional effect, specifically its light internally, but also because it plays to a possibility of using glass as an insulating material.[43]

After initially considering a translucent foam glass that could reproduce this effect,[44] RRP proposed to use multi-layered glass blocks as the main material for the building envelope.[45] In the outline proposals, the blocks are framed with aluminium profiles and set between the floor slabs of the structure to make the hierarchy between structure and envelope legible. (4.31). Yet due to the high dead weight and the bad insulation properties of glass blocks, this construction had to be rejected soon thereafter.[46]

During the design phase, RPP continued to pursue the idea of an envelope constructed from a multifunctional product that would provide both insulation and translucency. Instead of glass blocks, RRP sought a material

4.30 Photograph from Richard Rogers's article on the Maison de Verre by Pierre Chareau: the envelope made of glass blocks served as inspiration for the first designs of the Lloyd's Building.

similar to the German product Okalux, which the team had already used in small quantities in other projects. RRP was looking for a product comparable to the sandwich panels it had proposed to the glass-manufacturing company Pilkington in 'Notes on the Future of Glass',[47] so Pilkington was an obvious choice for a manufacturer. In a meeting in May 1979, representatives from Pilkington offered Davies and Young the prospect of developing glazing for the new building based on a triple glazing that Pilkington planned to launch in January. To achieve the translucent quality of the glazing, one of the panes was to be replaced with RRP-designed rolled patterned glass, for which Pilkington estimated the cost of an appropriately engraved roller at one thousand British pounds.[48]

To develop this proposal further, Pilkington and Young met again in September 1979 and discussed how to address both the optical and thermal requirements of the building envelope with the glazing. Young recorded the results of this meeting in one of his design notes (4.32a–b), which

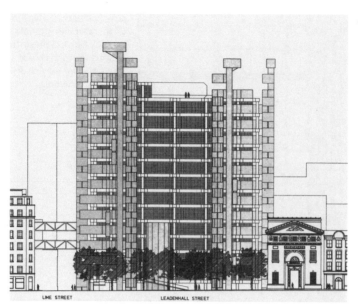

4.31 Outline design: elevation showing the envelope made of glass blocks

described the optical effect that the glazing should create inside and outside as the sparkle. This sparkle became one of the most important criteria in the search for glazing for the envelope. In a sketch on the design note that shows an exploded view of the glazing Young stipulated, a prismatic glass surface backed by a translucent vinyl layer produces this effect by both bundling and scattering light. Like the concrete construction joints in glass blocks, an egg-crate-like form in the space between the panes would prevent the increased glare that occurs with translucent surfaces. Young's sketch shows great similarities to a diagram of the polyvalent wall that Davies would later publish in his landmark article 'A Wall for All Seasons' in February 1981 (3.08). Both show the same novel principle of multi-layered glazing in which each individual layer fulfils a different function so the performance of the glazing can be extended at will.

The proposals that Pilkington sent Young following the meeting, however, were technically much more conservative than Young's sketch and were based on existing company products (4.33). In his response to Pilkington, written at the end of November 1979, Young stated the importance of the optical qualities of glass blocks for RRP. He stressed that the glazing must be structured on both the inside and outside so that the facade would sparkle at night from the artificial light inside the building. The surface structure of the glazing, which he suggested in an enclosed sketch, imitated a glass block structure with an orthogonal grid of lenses, each with a diameter of approximately thirty centimetres (4.34).

In addition to the optical properties and light transmission of the glazing, its thermal properties, especially the energy transmission, were the other important criteria for designing the building envelope. Because the external blinds to regulate solar radiation and energy transmission had to be dropped for cost reasons, RRP tested two glazing systems with Pilkington: one with an integrated shader and one with a vapour-deposited solar control coating. Both solutions converted absorbed solar radiation into heat. Depending on the degree of shielding and solar radiation, intense heat could build up in the space between the glass panes, leading to different thermal expansion and possible damages to the glazing.

To counteract the danger of heat accumulation, Young, after the meeting with Pilkington at which a multi-layered glazing was also discussed, considered in a sketch on the same design note (4.32a) a ventilated facade cavity that could dissipate excess heat. RRP may have known of the system of a ventilated facade from Banham's 1969 publication 'The Architecture of the Well-Tempered Environment',[49] in which he discussed Le Corbusier's work. Le Corbusier, who had termed the idea *mur neutralisant*, had proposed this type of system as early as 1930 for his Cité de Refuge project and had its thermal properties investigated at the St. Gobain company's laboratory (4.35). He never succeeded in convincing a client of the system, however, so he gave up on the proposal in 1947 after an additional unsuccessful proposal for the United Nations headquarters project in New York.[50] Independently of Le Corbusier's ideas, various companies developed exhaust air windows based on the principle of a ventilated space between panes after the 1950s.[51] The first patent for such an exhaust air window was registered in Sweden in 1956 and installed in a new building around ten years later.

At the beginning of the 1980s, several products for exhaust air windows existed in Scandinavia and the German-speaking world. Depending on the system, the exhaust air in the window was guided from bottom to top or top to bottom. While an exhaust air facade in summer removes the excess heat generated by solar radiation, in winter the warm exhaust air drawn through the cavity keeps the glass surface at approximately the same temperature as the interior. As a result, there is neither a drop in cold air nor heat radiation along the facade, so the thermal comfort in this zone is comparable to the surfaces inside a building. Although Young's idea of an exhaust air facade was first recorded in September 1979, this option was only pursued after the change of the climatic concept in May 1980.[52]

In June 1980, shortly before the completion of the scheme design report, Young outlined a more detailed axonometry of the exhaust air facade (4.36).[53]

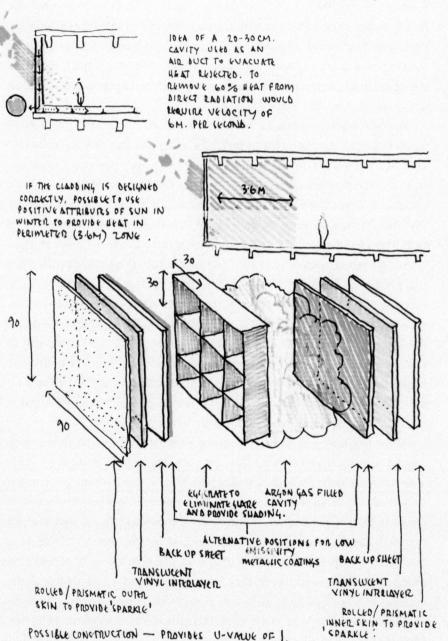

LLOYD'S   CLADDING

IDEAS BASED ON DISCUSSIONS WITH DAVID BUTTON + COLLEAGUE SEPT. 19 '79.
RAY JENNINGS.

IDEA OF A 20-30 CM.
CAVITY USED AS AN
AIR DUCT TO EVACUATE
HEAT REJECTED. TO
REMOVE 60% HEAT FROM
DIRECT RADIATION WOULD
REQUIRE VELOCITY OF
6M. PER SECOND.

IF THE CLADDING IS DESIGNED
CORRECTLY, POSSIBLE TO USE
POSITIVE ATTRIBUTES OF SUN IN
WINTER TO PROVIDE HEAT IN
PERIMETER (3.6M) ZONE.

3.6M

30
30

90
90

ELIMINATE TO
ELIMINATE GLARE
AND PROVIDE SHADING.

ARGON GAS FILLED
CAVITY

ALTERNATIVE POSITIONS FOR LOW
EMISSIVITY
METALLIC COATINGS

BACK UP SHEET

BACK UP SHEET

TRANSLUCENT
VINYL INTERLAYER

TRANSLUCENT
VINYL INTERLAYER

ROLLED / PRISMATIC OUTER
SKIN TO PROVIDE 'SPARKLE'

ROLLED / PRISMATIC
INNER SKIN TO PROVIDE
'SPARKLE'

POSSIBLE CONSTRUCTION — PROVIDES U-VALUE OF 1.

4.32a–b Design notes for the building envelope showing both the idea of the exhaust air facade
and that of a layered, multifunctional glazing panel, John Young, 23 September 1979

SKIN 4

6mm.   6mm.

THE COMPLETE ASSEMBLY ROUGHLY TO SCALE.
THE EGG CRATE IN THE CAVITY WOULD ELIMINATE
THE GLARE ASSOCIATED WITH ALL TRANSLUCENT WALLS AND
BEHAVE LIKE THE CONCRETE CONSTRUCTION JOINTS IN GLASS BLOCKS.
DEPENDING ON THE FRONT TO BACK DEPTH, IT COULD ALSO PROVIDE
SHADING, THUS ELIMINATING THE NEED FOR A SUMMER QUICK
RESPONSE COOLING SYSTEM, WHICH CAN ONLY BE DONE WITH AN
AIR/WATER SYSTEM AND IS THEREFORE BULKY. QUICK RESPONSE
HEAT SYSTEM FOR WINTER CAN BE TWO WATER PIPES ONLY.

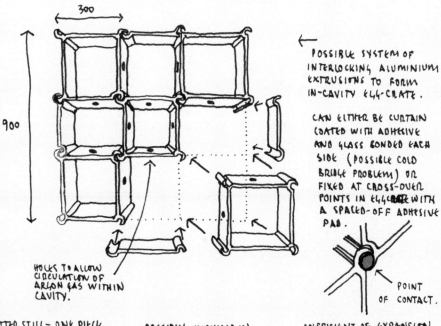

POSSIBLE SYSTEM OF
INTERLOCKING ALUMINIUM
EXTRUSIONS TO FORM
IN-CAVITY EGG-CRATE.

CAN EITHER BE CURTAIN
COATED WITH ADHESIVE
AND GLASS BONDED EACH
SIDE (POSSIBLE COLD
BRIDGE PROBLEM) OR
FIXED AT CROSS-OVER
POINTS IN EGG-CRATE WITH
A SPACED-OFF ADHESIVE
PAD.

POINT
OF CONTACT.

HOLES TO ALLOW
CIRCULATION OF
ARGON GAS WITHIN
CAVITY.

BETTER STILL - ONE PIECE
INJECTION MOULDING IN
SELF-SKINNING FOAM TO
GET STRENGTH, LIGHTNESS
AND INSIDE/OUTSIDE
THERMAL BREAK.

POSSIBLY MOULDED IN
ONE PIECE IN GRC, BUT
COLD BRIDGE PROBLEM
STILL EXISTS.

COEFFICIENT OF EXPANSION
MAY MAKE ALUMINIUM
INAPPROPRIATE?

JY 23/9/79.

107

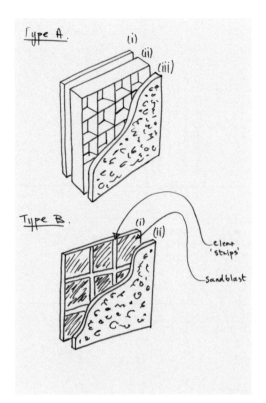

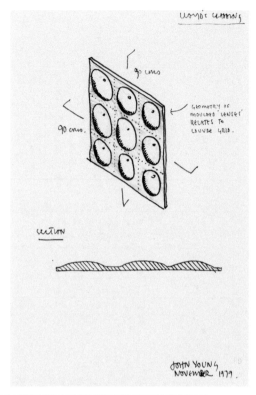

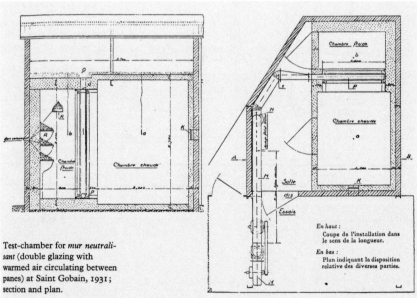

Test-chamber for *mur neutrali-sant* (double glazing with warmed air circulating between panes) at Saint Gobain, 1931; section and plan.

4.33 Sketches of possible glazing panel for the Lloyd's Building, Pilkington, October 1979

4.34 Sketch of structured glass with lenses approximately 30 centimetres in diameter, John Young, November 1979

4.35 Illustration showing the test chamber for Le Corbusier's mur neutralisant at Saint-Gobain, 1931

Following the logic of the system of a multifunctional, layered glazing in Young's sketch, (4.32a), the exhaust airflow in the facade cavity was just an additional layer that took on one of the functions of a dynamic envelope. Even though the exhaust air facade for the Lloyd's Building was still a long way from Davies' ideal of a polyvalent wall, Davies later saw it as an approach toward a construction element that was part of the building services and could react dynamically to changing conditions, thus coming one step closer to the idea of the intelligent environment.[54]

In the scheme design report, completed in June 1980, the glazing was finally described as follows:

> Cladding to the main superstructure will be constructed from triple glazed units comprising solar control and low emissivity coatings. Extract air will be drawn through the inner cavity to reduce heat transfer between the coupled space and outside and to collect some of the solar energy falling on the facade.[55]
>
> The glass panels will have a crystal pattern rolled in during the manufacturing process to reflect light, bringing sparkle and colour to the external wall in the daytime and at night.[56]

The glass panes were held by a profile system of dark anodised aluminium frames whose divisions would be determined by the structure. While the vertical division would be based on the 1.8-metre module of the beam grid, the horizontal division would have to accommodate the height of the bracket, which at this stage of the design still penetrated the facade's glazing. Detailed drawings of the glazing system show an I-beam mullion composed of individual aluminium profiles, the outer glass panes fixed with glazing beads. The thermal break of the mullions was made of synthetic material. An inner and an outer glazing, separated by a profile, formed the facade cavity (4.37a–b).

While in the scheme design report RRP described the exhaust air facade as a means of reducing overheating in summer, Ove Arup & Partners only highlighted the improved comfort along the facade in winter as an advantage of this system in its report on the new air conditioning system.[57] Ove Arup & Partners let Pilkington's Environmental Advisory Service investigate the effects of the exhaust air facade on solar radiation and energy transmission in March 1981. The expected surface temperature of the inner pane was calculated using a simple mathematical model for various types of protective coatings (4.38a–c). The calculations showed that the effect of the

(A) BRINGS SUPPLY AIR INTO CENTRE OF EACH STRUCTURAL BAY, SPLITTING THE RETURN AIR COLLECTION DUCT BENEATH THE GLAZING IN TWO. ONE SUPPLY AIR CENTRAL AND TWO RETURN AIR AT ENDS PER BAY CONFLICTS WITH MAINTENANCE CRADLE THRU'WAY.

(B) BRINGS SUPPLY AIR IN AT ONE END OF EACH STRUCTURAL BAY, WITH BELOW GLAZING RETURN AIR DUCT EXHAUSTED FROM ONE END ONLY. ONE SUPPLY AIR AND ONE RETURN AIR BRANCH AT THE END OF EACH BAY LEAVES A GENEROUS CENTRAL ZONE FOR MAINTENANCE CRADLE ACCESS.

CONCLUSION — PURSUE (B) BUT CHECK WITH ARUPS FOR AIRFLOWS ETC.

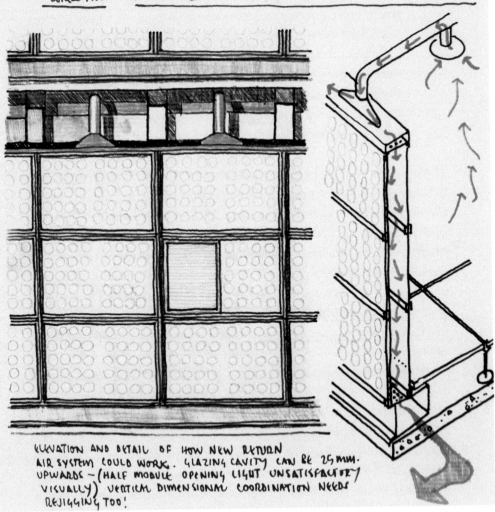

ELEVATION AND DETAIL OF HOW NEW RETURN AIR SYSTEM COULD WORK. GLAZING CAVITY CAN BE 25 MM. UPWARDS — (HALF MODULE OPENING LIGHT UNSATISFACTORY VISUALLY) VERTICAL DIMENSIONAL COORDINATION NEEDS REJIGGING TOO!

4.36 Design note on the exhaust air facade: the openable window sash only fills half of a module so as not to block the airflow. John Young, 1 June 1980

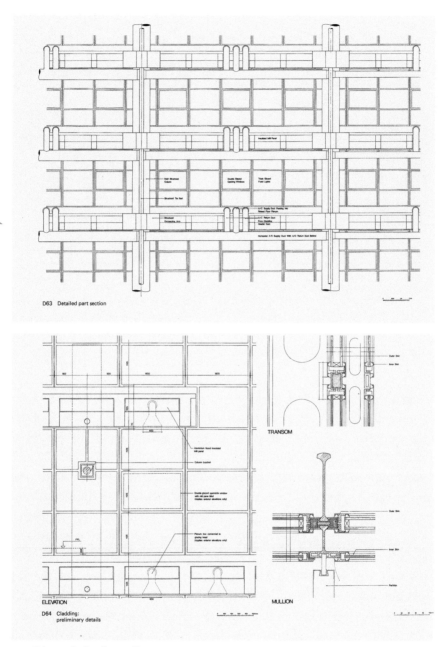

D63   Detailed part section

ELEVATION

TRANSOM

MULLION

D64   Cladding:
preliminary details

4.37 Scheme design, June 1980

a Facade elevation showing the tie-down system
b Details and elevation of building envelope showing the connection to the bracket penetration

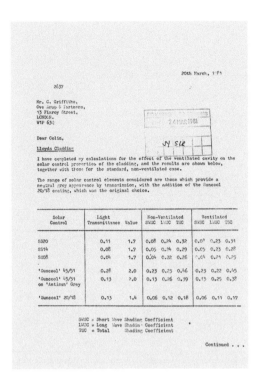

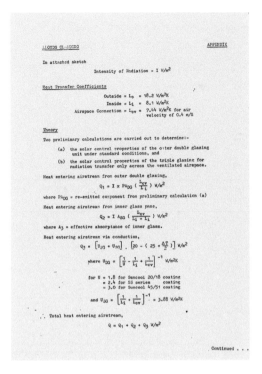

exhaust air facade on absorbing the solar radiation was negligible. The benefit seemed to be limited to the situation in winter. The calculation method was then discussed in a meeting, where interpretation of the results diverged: 'During winter – low sun elevation – the shading coefficient is significantly improved. Overall improvement due to ventilated cavity varies between ±5 to ±25 per cent. Disagreement arose between RJ [Pilkington] and CG [OAP] since both chose figures at opposite ends of the performance range.'[58] Various diagrams by RRP (4.39, 4.40) and Ove Arup & Partners (4.41a–b, 4.42), which describe the effect of ventilation on building physics in more detail, suggest that the calculations were revised later and the two positions thus came closer together. Yet there was no reliable or sufficiently accurate physical model to determine the effects of ventilation by pure calculation. Thus, the question remained of how well the proposed exhaust air facade would perform.

For the proposed building envelope system to be implemented, three technical issues needed to be solved. First, the embossed pattern for producing the sparkly effect and the sun protection coating had to be determined for the patterned glass, and a low-cost manufacturing process with small pattern deviations had to be developed. Second, for the exhaust air system to fulfil its function, it was necessary to work out an even air distribution

Substituting for various values of L etc. gives

$$Q = I (0.92 \ FA_{DG} + 0.46 \ A_{SG})$$
$$- 0.5 (10 + \Delta T) (U_{DG} + 3.88) \ Watts/m^2$$

for 1.8 x 3.0 m module, total heat inspect

$$Q = 3.0 \times 1.8 \times Q = 5.4 \ Q \ Watts$$

Heat carried away by airstream in 1.8 x 3.0 m module for v = 0.4 m/s

$$= Volume \times Density \times Sp. Heat \times \Delta T$$
$$= 0.07 \times 1.8 \times 0.4 \times 1.17 \times 1000 \times \Delta T$$
$$= 58.97 \ T$$

This also equals Q

∴ Equating for Q we get

$$\Delta T = \frac{(4.97 \ FA_{DG} + 2.48 \ A_{SG}) I - 27 \ U_{DG} - 104.76}{2.7 \ U_{DG} + 69.45}$$

From this can be obtained the heat entering the conditioned space from the airspace. This has to be added to the results of preliminary calculation (b) above.

The attached graph shows the results of evaluating the gain from the airspace for a range of radiation intensities. The two lines plotted define the range of results.

4.38a–c Calculations on the effect of the ventilated cavity on energy transmission by radiation, Pilkington, 20 March 1981

in the cavity that would also bypass the openable window, determine the temperature and condensation behaviour at the surface of the glazing in relation to the speed and temperature of the airflow, and it was necessary to find a way to open the ventilated cavity for cleaning. Finally, constructing and smoothly assembling the building envelope required addressing problems regarding the penetration detail of the ceiling support, the deflection of the mullions under horizontal load, the assembly sequence of the facade and the tolerance compensation for assembly and movement deviations.

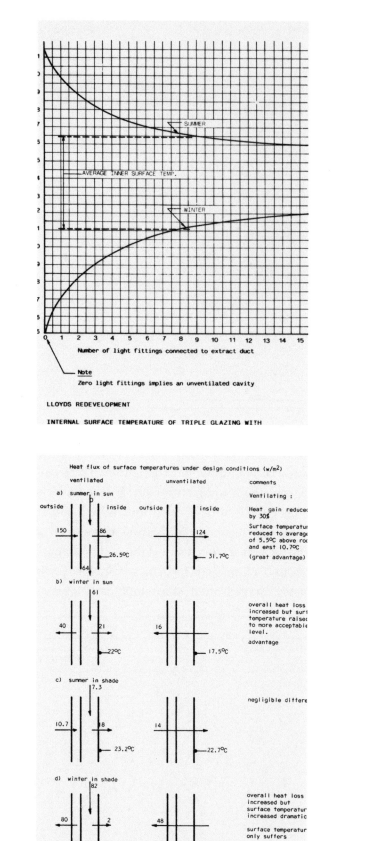

Number of light fittings connected to extract duct

Note
Zero light fittings implies an unventilated cavity

LLOYDS REDEVELOPMENT

INTERNAL SURFACE TEMPERATURE OF TRIPLE GLAZING WITH

Heat flux of surface temperatures under design conditions (w/m²)

ventilated   unventilated   comments

a) summer in sun   Ventilating :

outside   inside   outside   inside   Heat gain reduced
                                             by 30%

150   86   124   Surface temperature
         26.5°C   31.7°C   reduced to average
                                         of 5.5°C above roo
         64   and east 10.7°C

                                         (great advantage)

b) winter in sun   overall heat loss
         61   increased but surf
                                         temperature raised
40   21   16   to more acceptable
         22°C   17.5°C   level.

                                         advantage

c) summer in shade   negligible differe
         7.3
10.7   18   14
         23.2°C   22.7°C

d) winter in shade   overall heat loss
         82   increased but
80   2   48   surface temperatur
         21.3   15°C   increased dramatic

                                         surface temperatur
                                         only suffers

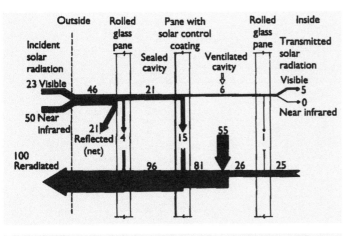

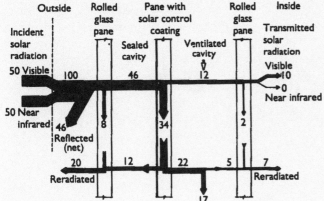

4.39 Inner surface temperature of the glazing as a function of the number of lighting fittings connected to the extract duct, RRP

4.40 Effect of the ventilated cavity on heat gain and loss under various conditions, RRP

4.41a–b Predicted heat loss and gain through the exhaust air facade for worst case scenarios in (a) winter and (b) summer, Ove Arup & Partners

4.42 Effect of the exhaust air facade on the room temperature in summer and winter, Ove Arup & Partners, June 1981

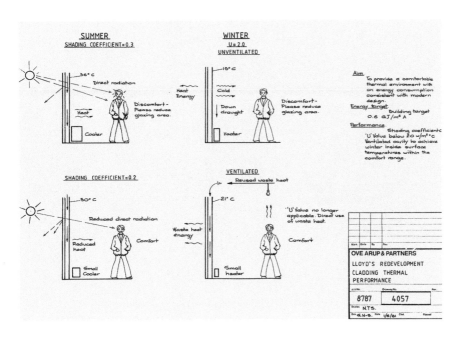

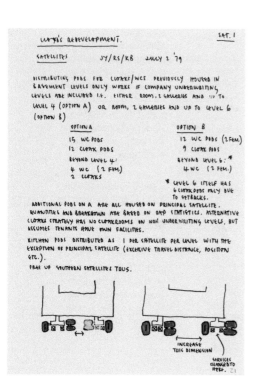

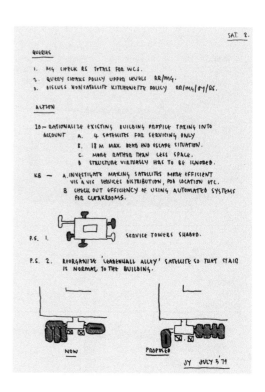

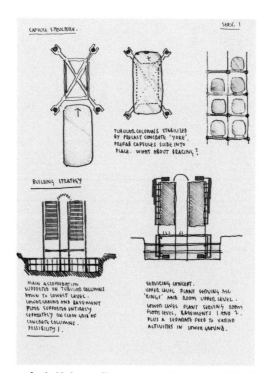

4.43a–c Design notes for (a, b) the satellite towers, 2 July 1979, and (c) their structure, John Young, 1 September 1979

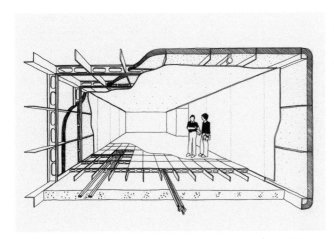

4.44 Cutaway drawing of a capsule for the 'Tower Capsule Manufacturing/Fabricators Briefing Guide', RRP, December 1979

4.45 Early drawing of toilet capsule, fire escape stairs and lift link, RRP

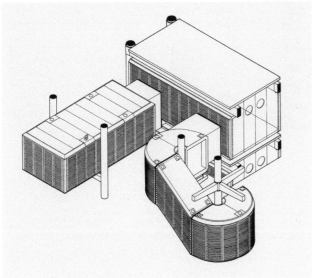

Satellite and capsules

In parallel with the main building, the structure and the servant elements of the satellite towers were designed (4.43a–4.46). In contrast to the main building, which was largely manufactured in situ, the degree of prefabrication here was to be as high as possible due to the restrictive space conditions on the construction site and the tight schedule.

For the capsules, Richard Rogers + Partners compiled a 'Manufacturing/ Fabricators Briefing Guide' at the end of 1979.[59] This did not have the status of tender documents but was probably intended to explore the feasibility of the designed construction and the corresponding costs. The prices offered by the various manufacturers were far above the budgeted costs, however, probably due to the high risks that the construction industry manufacturers

4.46 Early model of a satellite tower with servant elements, RRP

attributed to this unconventional project.[60] Ultimately, the industrial engineering group of Ove Arup & Partners was commissioned to build, in close cooperation with manufacturers from the plant's construction sector, a prototype of the capsule to clarify any initial technical issues and then produce a series of thirty-three capsules. The aim was to find a construction with an inexpensive manufacturing process and whose assembled weight was below the load limits of the available construction cranes. The dynamic and static load-bearing behaviour and the assembly process of the cell would still have to be tested.

Open Promises

The reconstruction of the design process for the Lloyd's Building shows how RRP met the complex requirements with a concept design that raised many critical technical questions. RRP's design approached the question of how Lloyd's could solve its problems over the next fifty years not with a solution but a promise. The design of the nucleus of the Lloyd's market, the Room where underwriters and brokers meet, promised a visionary building that would meet all the needs of a modern working world: the Omniplatz.[61]

At this stage, the designed building was still more an architectural vision than a realistic construction project. With its design, RRP shifted the complex problems of the job away from architectural issues toward the technical level of construction. Following the principle of legibility, elements were to be left visible and very high quality, but striving to align these principles raised further technical questions. The British construction industry did not offer ready-made solutions for such problems, so executing the project would entail numerous risks. The following chapter is devoted to the measures taken to minimize these risks.

1   Banham, 'The Quality of Modernism', 56.
2   Richard Rogers + Partners, 'Lloyd's: Outline Proposals Report', June 1979, Archive RSHP, London.
3   Richard Rogers + Partners, 'Lloyd's: Scheme Design Development Report', June 1980, Archive RSHP, London.
4   Richard Rogers + Partners, 'Lloyd's: Detail Design Development Report', June 1982, Archive RSHP, London.
5   Cf. Richard Rogers + Partners, 'Lloyd's: Outline Proposals', 1.
6   Richard Rogers + Partners, 'Lloyd's: Detail Design'.
7   Piano + Rogers Architects, 'A Design Strategy for Lloyd's'.
8   Cf. Richard Rogers + Partners, 'Lloyd's: Outline Proposals', 2.
9   Cf. Richard Rogers + Partners, 'Lloyd's: Outline Proposals', 27–8.
10 Cf. Richard Rogers + Partners, 'Lloyd's: Outline Proposals', 2.
11 Cf. Meredith L. Clausen, 'Frank Lloyd Wright, Vertical Space, and the Chicago School's Quest for Light', *Journal of the Society of Architectural Historians* 44, no. 1 (1985), 66–74.
12 Cf. Banham, *Architecture of the Well-Tempered*, 86–92; Reyner Banham, 'The Services of the Larkin "a" Building', *Journal of the Society of Architectural Historians* 37, no. 3 (1978), 195–7.
13 Cf. Francis Duffy, 'Bürolandschaft '58–'78', *The Architectural Review* CLXV, no. 983 (1979), 54–8.
14 For example, the Southdale Centre, one of the first malls designed by Victor Gruen in the late 1950s.
15 Reyner Banham, 'Louis Kahn: The Buttery-Hatch Aesthetic', *The Architectural Review* 131, no. 781 (1962), 205f.
16 Richard Rogers + Partners, 'Lloyd's: Outline Proposals', 2.
17 Colin Davies, 'The "Omniplatz"', *Architectural Review* 180, no. 1076 (1986), 60.
18 Cf. Piano + Rogers Architects, 'A Design Strategy for Lloyd's', 24–5 and 60–2.
19 Cf. Ove Arup & Partners, 'A Proposal for the Air-Conditioning of the Superstructure', 1980, Archive Arup, London, 2.
20 Ove Arup & Partners, 'Proposal for the Air-Conditioning' 2.
21 Cf. Ove Arup & Partners, 'Proposal for the Air-Conditioning'.
22 In January 1979, Tom Barker had judged this type of airflow over a hollow floor to be unfavourable, which is why it was not pursued further at that time. Cf. 'Design Team Meeting Minutes', 1978–1981, Archive RSHP, London, 187.
23 Cf. Franc Sodec and Richard Craig, 'The Underfloor Air Supply System: The European Experience', in *ASHRAE Transactions* 96 (1990), 690–5.
24 Cf. Kurt Brandle and Robert F. Boehm, 'Evaluation of Air-Flow Windows: Final Report' (Lawrence Berkeley Laboratory, University of California, 1981), A8.
25 Cf. Ove Arup & Partners, 'Proposal for the Air-Conditioning', 8.

26 The role of the engineers involved – especially that of Rice – has not been fully clarified. Since the completion of the Centre Pompidou, Rice had no longer worked exclusively for Ove Arup & Partners but had pursued his own projects together with Piano. In the report to the selection process, he is listed before Ove Arup & Partners as an additional consulting engineer. The responsible engineer at Ove Arup & Partners was John Roberts. John Thornton seems to have taken over this role later.

27 Peter Rice quotations from 'Technical Notes', 1979–1980, Archive RSHP, London, 221.

28 Cf. Richard Rogers + Partners, 'Lloyd's: Outline Proposals', 38.

29 Rice and Thornton, 'Lloyd's Redevelopment', 269.

30 A beam grid consists of two sets of beams in one plane, which cross each other at right, acute or obtuse angles. The beams are rigidly connected to each other at crossing points. Cf. Zygmunt Stanislaw Makowski, *Steel Space Structures* (London: Michael Joseph, 1965), 12.

31 Cf. Makowski, *Steel Space Structures*.

32 This stage of the design was presented by Rogers in an audio-visual talk. Cf. Richard Rogers, 'Genesis of the New Lloyd's Underwriting Room' (Pidgeon Audiovisual, 1979).

33 Cf. Rice and Thornton, 'Lloyd's Redevelopment', 269.

34 See 'Design for Better Assembly: (5) Case Study: Rogers' and Arup's', *Architects' Journal* 180, no. 36 (1984), 87–94.

35 Cf. Peter Rice, 'Technical Notes', 1979–1980, Archive RSHP, London, 221.

36 This status of the project was published in 'Projekt für die Lloyd's Versicherer in London', *Werk, Bauen + Wohnen* 67, no. 4 (1980), 14–27, and 'Architecture and the Programme'.

37 Cf. Rice and Thornton, 'Lloyd's Redevelopment', 269 and 271.

38 Rice and Thornton, 'Lloyd's Redevelopment', 269.

39 Cf. Geoffrey Ashworth, 'Computers Take on the Lloyd's Challenge', *Building* CCL, no. 7443 (1986), 55–7.

40 Rice and Thornton, 'Lloyd's Redevelopment', 269.

41 'Coordination Meeting Minutes', 1980–1981, Archive RSHP, London, 138.

42 Peter Rice, *An Engineer Imagines* (London: Artemis, 1994), 79.

43 Rogers, 'Genesis'.

44 'Pilkington File',1978–1982, Archive RSHP, London.

45 Richard Rogers + Partners, 'Lloyd's: Outline Proposals', 56.

46 Email from Klaus Wertz, 3 December 2015.

47 Cf. pages 46–50.

48 'Pilkington File', Archive RSHP, 51.

49 Cf. Banham, *Architecture of the Well-Tempered*, 156 ff.

50 Harvey J. Bryan, 'Le Corbusier and the "Mur Neutralisant": An Early Example in Double Envelope Construction', in Servando Alvarez et al., eds., *Architecture and Urban Space*, International PLEA Organisation; (Dordrecht: Kluwer, 1991), 257–62.

51 Cf. the history of development of exhaust air windows, Brandle and Boehm, 'Evaluation of Air-Flow Windows', A1.

52 Cf. page 67.

53 Richard Rogers + Partners, 'Lloyd's John Young's Design Notes' (London, 1979–1980), 37–38.

54 Davies, 'The Design of the Intelligent Environment', 165.

55 Richard Rogers + Partners, 'Lloyd's: Scheme Design', 47.

56 Richard Rogers + Partners, 'Lloyd's: Scheme Design', 84.

57 Ove Arup & Partners, 'Proposal for the Air-Conditioning', 6.

58 'Pilkington File', Archive RSHP.

59 Richard Rogers + Partners, 'Lloyd's: Tower Capsule, Manufacturing + Fabricators Briefing Guide', December 1979, Archive RSHP, London.

60 John Roberts, 'Sanitary Connections: A Case History of Innovation', *Arup Journal* 19, no. 3 (1984), 24–7.

61 Davies, 'The "Omniplatz"'.

5. Framing the Risk

> We are in the risk business, so why shouldn't we take one more?[1]
> Courtenay Blackmore, Head of Lloyd's Administration

The design team from Richard Rogers + Partners (RRP) and Ove Arup & Partners met the challenging requirements from Lloyd's for a building that would meet its needs in the long term by basing the design on the ideas of the megastructure, the intelligent environment and the principle of legibility. The visionary design relied on a series of novel constructive and technical propositions that allowed for shifting the complex problems of the design away from architectural toward engineering issues. These novelties were decisive for the successful implementation of the design and the subsequent operation of the building – but they also entailed both unidentified and new types of risks for which the probability of negative outcomes and their potential severity were unknown.

Negative consequences of risk in the construction process tend to affect three core factors of a project: deadlines, costs and performance, which result in delays, cost overruns and technical, functional or aesthetic project deficiencies. It is the constitutive task of planning – and thus also within the scope of expertise of the members of the design team, be they architects or engineers – to develop and organise a process whose steps allow the design at hand to be executed without provoking risks. Risks must therefore already be identified during the design and minimised as far as possible.

For conventional, traditional constructions and technologies, architects and engineers are aware of most of the risks that may occur during construction or afterward and have developed discipline-specific methods and tools to avert them. Novel construction and technologies, on the other hand, entail types of risks that have not yet been assessed or that may even be unknown. The design team from RRP and Ove Arup & Partners had already considered how to deal with such novel ideas in their report for the selection process:

> At a detailed level we must identify the elements which influence the risk being taken. Specifically, we must be guided by past experience and not assume that a quantum improvement can be achieved. Some improvements on current practice can be made and it is fair to say that construction in Britain has often not appeared to learn from

progress made abroad. A certain part of this reticence to learn from foreign experience has been because of the nature of the management/union relationship. Prudently then we should plan for a reasonable improvement of the best current practice and only embark on novel ideas after thorough research.[2]

Lloyd's decided, based on these considerations and the recommendation of the design team, to take two exceptional measures: to involve a management contractor in the organisation of the design team and to implement a mock-up programme under the contractor's management. Both measures were crucial for assessing and minimising the risks of the proposed novelties.

Management Contracting

Management contracting, a 'way of getting buildings built',[3] became popular in England around 1980 but had been developing there since the 1920s in response to the disadvantages of the typical general contractor approach (5.01, 5.02). Bovis Construction Ltd., commissioned as the management contractor for the Lloyd's Building, was already a key player in elaborating and propagating this form of construction procurement. The emergence of management contracting out of the traditional general contractor approach demonstrates its advantages and disadvantages and its influence on the way a building project is designed and built.[4]

The concept of the general contractor, solely responsible for the execution of a construction project, first appeared in Great Britain in connection with the large infrastructure buildings of the eighteenth century. New types of engineering structures, such as lighthouse or bridges, could not be built by the traditional trades that specialised in building construction. Instead, the general contractor, willing to address problems that arose in the implementation of these daring projects, was appointed to bear the client's risk by being directly responsible for each of the trade's sub-contractors, thus solving the challenges of collaboration between various professionals and tradespeople.

After this type of project organisation had established itself in civil engineering, contractors began to appear in the field of more typical building construction at the beginning of the nineteenth century. One of the most successful was Thomas Cubitt (1788–1855), who built many large residential complexes in London (including Bellgravia and Pimlico) and was responsible for the main facade of Buckingham Palace. Originally a carpenter, at the beginning of his career he entered contracts with other tradespeople (master

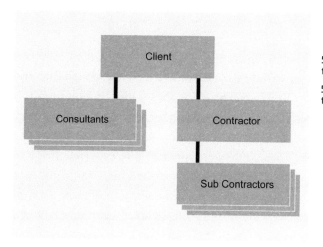

5.01 Traditional contractor system

5.02 Management con-
tractor system

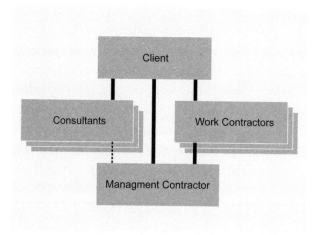

builders, carpenters, plumbers, etc.) to build houses under a lump-sum contract. Later, he began to gradually integrate these skills into his company by
directly hiring craftsmen, engineers and architects. In this way he expanded his range of services, becoming both an investor and total contractor. At
the peak of his career, he employed a thousand workers, produced his own
building materials, developed sites with his design department and granted
loans to support development.

From England, the contractor's model expanded to the United States.
Many of the complex and tall office buildings built in Chicago and New York
since 1870 were built through contractors. Among them, George A. Fuller's
company, responsible for the construction of buildings such as the
Monadnock Building, the Tacoma Building, the Rookery Building and the
Flatiron Building, stands out. Fuller, a trained architect, took an early interest in construction problems and specialised in, among other things, fire-
proof steel – a key technology for the buildings concerned. From 1881 on, he

offered his expertise as a general contractor, thus relieving the burden on architects who no longer wished to take on the heavy responsibility and organisational effort involved in constructing these complex buildings.

Project expertise was not the only condition for a successful contractor – a contractor also had to have sufficient capital to cover costs until the first remuneration by the client. These sums were considerable, especially for large projects where the contractor had to pay for supplied material in advance. Fuller addressed this problem with the cost-plus contract, which he used for the first time in the Rookery Building (1886–1888) of Burnham & Root.[5] The project included contractual elements that found their way into British building culture through management contracting one hundred years later. Under a cost-plus contract, the contractor receives a fee for coordinating, organizing and carrying out the project, while the client pays the resulting costs. In contrast to a lump-sum contract, the contractor in a cost-plus contract is responsible for organisation but not the building construction itself.

While the cost-plus contract model arose out of the contractor's predicament, it also has advantages for clients and architects: since construction work is subcontracted to various companies according to the progress of the design, cost-plus contracts make it possible to start work as soon as the work package for a trade – not for the whole building as with a lump-sum contract – is specified. This allows the contractor to run design and construction partially side by side, thus shortening the time needed to realize the building. As early as the 1920s, Bovis in London offered a form of project organisation derived from Fuller's cost-plus contract. Called the Bovis System, it was first used in 1927 in a contract with the retailer Marks & Spencer (5.03). Bovis was awarded a fixed fee for its services, with a bonus in the event of savings. Bovis would be compensated for the actual construction costs incurred, and Marks & Spencer would benefit from the savings.[6]

In both the cost-plus contract and the Bovis System, the authority that organises the work of the trades receives a stated fee. In contrast, in general contracting, this profit is earned via a hidden margin in the price of the work. Since Bovis was still responsible for constructing the individual work packages, it was faced with the dilemma of having to act between the interests of the client, to whom it was obliged as a professional, and its own commercial interests within the contract's framework for the work packages. To overcome this conflict of interest, Bovis invented the management contract for the construction of the new cigarette factory for John Player & Sons in Nottingham by Arup Associates in 1968. Under this type of contract, Bovis no longer executed construction work, instead assuming the role of a service

Articles of Agreement

Jno Luther Green

28 OCT 1927

5.03 Agreement between Marks & Spencer and Bovis on an early form management contracting, 1926

made the   day of   One

thousand nine hundred and   B E T W E E N

Messrs. MARKS & SPENCER, Limited, of No. 21 Chiswell

Street, London, E.C.2. (hereinafter called "the Employer")

of the one part and Messrs. BOVIS, Limited, of 47 Upper

Berkeley Street, London, W.1. (hereinafter called "the

Contractor") of the other part   WHEREAS   the Employer

is desirous of

and has caused Drawings and a Specification describing

the work to be done to be prepared by

AND WHEREAS the said Drawings numbered

and the Specification and the Bills of

Quantities have been signed by or on behalf of the parties

hereto AND WHEREAS the Contractor has agreed to execute

upon and subject to the conditions set forth and the

Schedules attached hereto the work shewn upon the said

Drawings and described in the said Specification and

included in the said Bills of Quantities for a Fee to be

paid to him and the refund of the prime cost thereof as

defined in the Schedules "A", "B" and "C" hereto.

NOW IT IS HEREBY AGREED AS FOLLOWS :-

1.   IN consideration of the Fee above referred to and

of the refund of the prime cost of the works to be paid

at the times and in the manner set forth in the said

Conditions the Contractor will upon and subject to the

said Conditions execute and complete the work shewn upon

the said Drawings and described in the said Specification

and Bills of Quantities.

2.   THE Employer will pay the Contractor the said Fee

and refund the prime cost or such other sum as shall become

payable hereunder at the times and in the manner specified

provider. Because a management contractor is remunerated on a mutually agreed fee, work can be done in the interests of the client without having to earn profit via hidden margins, as is often the case with contractors.

Management contracting presents advantages, above all for complex and time-critical projects (as the Lloyd's Building would prove to be): since the construction work is split into individual work packages, the construction can begin as soon as the tender for demolition and excavation has been submitted. In the general contractor model, the design would already have to be completed by this time, as the tendering process includes all work packages. This newly possible overlapping of design and construction can enable earlier occupation of the building or a longer design phase. Another important advantage of organizing the construction work with a management contractor is the early involvement of the building experts in the design. Complex

5.04 The Lloyd's design team with its client, early 1980s (from left to right): Geoff Ashworth (MDA), John Young (RRP), Sir Peter Green (Chairman of Lloyd's), Marco Goldschmied (RRP), Peter Rice (Ove Arup & Partners), Richard Rogers, Mike Davies (RRP), Courtney Blackmore (Head of Lloyd's Administration), Brian Pettifer (Bovis), Nick Ayres (MDA), John Smith (Bovis). Not pictured are John Bathgate, the Lloyd's project coordinator, and Tom Barker (Ove Arup & Partners).

5.05 Organigram of the project organisation, retrospectively created, Courtenay Blackmore
5.06 List of meetings with persons involved and chairmen

projects can benefit greatly from their knowledge of manufacturing processes, construction technologies and the associated risks. However, involving a management contractor too early can also be disadvantageous: the contractor's building expertise risks heightened preferences for standardised or proven solutions over novel ones, thus restricting the design process.

As a management contractor, Bovis typically joined a design team during the design, supported it in construction matters and created the various tender packages together with it. Additionally, Bovis assumed responsible for scheduling and site organisation, including site management. The work contractors and suppliers were selected in a competitive procedure, whereby the client decided whom to award each contract.[7] The management contractor then concluded contracts with the work contractors, charging the client directly for the costs, and coordinated and supervised their work. For its services, the management contractor received a fee of 1.5–2.5 per cent of the building costs.[8] After the factory for John Players & Sons, Bovis successfully completed several other projects under a management contract. These included major projects such as the Willis Faber & Dumas

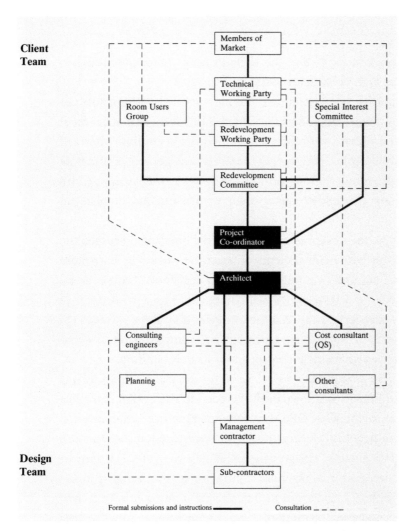

Client Team

- Members of Market
- Technical Working Party
- Room Users Group
- Redevelopment Working Party
- Special Interest Committee
- Redevelopment Committee
- Project Co-ordinator
- Architect
- Consulting engineers
- Cost consultant (QS)
- Planning
- Other consultants
- Management contractor

Design Team

- Sub-contractors

Formal submissions and instructions ■■■■■   Consultation _ _ _ _

LLOYD'S REDEVELOPMENT

Meetings (* denotes chairman/minute taker)

	LLOYD'S	RRP	OAP	OAP PPSS	MDA	BOVIS
Redevelopment Committee	PG CB* JB	RR MG PD	PR TB		GA	BP
Redevelopment Working Party	CB* JB	RR MG PD	PR TB JR		GA NA	BP
Technical Working Party	JB PN	JY* PD	JR		NA	
Coordination meeting	JB	JY GA*	JR FM	HS	NA	BP JS JW
Redevelopment Users' Group	CB* JF	MG PD				
Cost Review	JB	JY	JR		NA	JW*
Design Progress		JY GA	JR TR	HS	NA AH	JW MD JS*
Site Meeting		MG* CW	JR MB TR	PB	NA	BP JS
Monday mid-day Meeting		RR MG JY*RS	PR TB JR CG		NA GA	(JS BP)
RRP Design Meeting		RR MG JY RS				
Boxes Working Group	JF AR	MG MD PD				
Strategy Meeting	CB JB	RR* (JY MG)	PR TB		GA	BP
Boxes Development Group	CB* JF AR	MG MD PD				
Services/Building Automation Systems	JB* BB IM		JR MH			

Building in Ipswich in 1975 and the Renault spare parts warehouse in Swindon in 1982, both by Norman Foster.[9]

Due to its expertise, Bovis remained without much competition until the end of the 1970s. Many companies that entered this form of management contracting had problems with their new role in the beginning, often falling back on familiar roles, conducting themselves as general contractors motivated by profit rather than supporting the design team. It was not until the early 1980s that the field of management contracting providers began to expand.[10]

In August 1979, the design team of the Lloyd's Building discussed the ideal time to involve the management contractor to 'make the maximum contribution without unduly influencing design decisions.'[11] After several rounds of interviews, a shortlist of five companies was agreed upon in December 1979: Mowlem, Laing, Wimpey, Bovis and Trollope + Colls.[12] On 13 May 1980, shortly before the scheme design was completed, Lloyd's finally engaged Bovis as management contractor for its new building.[13]

In mid-1980, the new project organisation for the Lloyd's Building was implemented and Bovis was henceforth included in the design team as a management contractor (5.04, 5.05). It contributed expertise mainly through two types of meetings: RRP-chaired design and construction coordination meetings and Bovis-chaired design progress meetings (5.06). The early involvement of Bovis as a management contractor in the design process aligned with both how Lloyd's and RRP dealt with unknowns within their business models and working methods. Various specialists – as with Bovis as a contractor – were included in the dialogue to identify risks and avert them by finding optimal solutions together as a team.

Planning the Investigation

One of the first measures taken in the collaboration with the newly appointed management contractor Bovis was the launch of an extensive mock-up programme.[14] All open questions that resulted from the architectural concept and the technical system were to be investigated and eventually answered both to handle the associated risks and to stay true to the design team's visionary design. To this end, the overall construction programme included the implementation of two mock-ups: one for a corner section of one full storey of the building – later simply called Mock-Up One by the design team – and one for a toilet capsule for the satellite tower. Bovis set the deadlines for the mock-up programme while Ove Arup & Partners and RRP provided the specifications, which were approved by Lloyd's in December, 1980.[15]

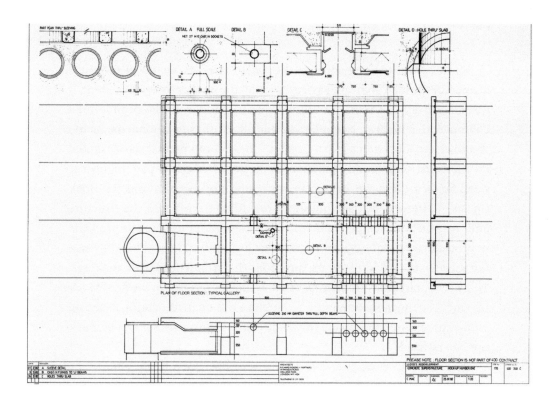

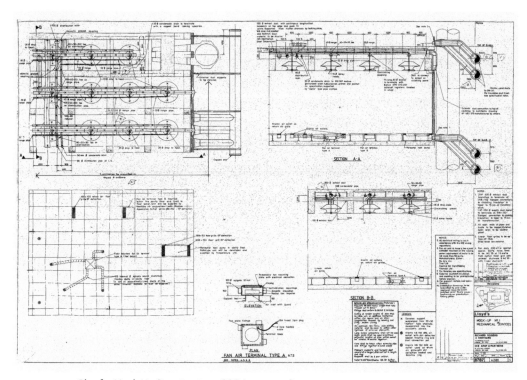

5.07   Plan for Mock-Up One structure, RRP, January 1982

5.08   Plan for mechanical services for Mock-Up One, November 1981, Ove Arup & Partners

Mock-Up One mainly addressed the constructive and technical questions created by the idea of the megastructure and the intelligent environment. It was comprised of a section of three-by-four modules of the beam grid, a column with a bracket, a ventilated facade and fully operational mechanical and electrical systems (5.07, 5.08). All these components were essential for the construction and operation of the series of clear span, highly serviced floors around the atrium. In particular, the specifications for Mock-Up One addressed the open questions regarding the services, the structure and the envelope. Instead of defining the requirements (such as products or procedures) for these parts of the building, as would usually be the case, the specifications addressed the questions that would need to be answered. This necessitated the production of other mock-ups prior to the final Mock-Up One. The mock-up programme therefore was an investigation based on empirical research that made use of the various purposes for which mock-ups can be used.

Several detailed studies were planned for the concrete mix, shuttering design and beam grid 'to establish which construction method is the most suitable and to establish the quality of workmanship and finish that can reasonably be expected'.[16] Further, the mock-up programme aimed to investigate the development of the column bracket assembly; the ventilated facade and its methods of jointing, finishes and assembly; and the glass type, size, availability and physical properties. Other studies were scheduled for the cavity floor, the ductwork and the building services equipment that 'may be run continuously for an extended interval and the same tests carried out again to determine reliability and long-term performance.'[17] Several points of the specification implicitly programmed the collaboration between designers, engineers, fabricators and manufacturer to find optimal solutions and to obtain specifications for the tender before the assembly of the final mock-up. The programme aimed for an iterative testing and refinement process of Mock-Up One:

> The engineer will specify the environmental tests to be carried out such as temperature, humidity, noise levels, lighting levels, etc. ... on the basis of the results the architect may require modifications, followed by re-testing. ... after the initial commissioning and testing of the mock-up, Lloyd's approval should be sought before the superstructure construction goes ahead.[18]

The specification for Mock-Up One shows how the design focus shifted away from conception toward constructive and technical questions. While the focus in the previous design process was on technical systems such as the services, structure and envelope, the mock-up programme focussed on questions regarding components such as the beam grid, the ventilated facade or the glazing. The mock-up programme was not simply the next stage in the design process toward the final project but a new order of the design process ruled by constructive and technical criteria. This allowed the design team to move its focus to the risks of construction and building operation.

1   Appleyard, *The New Lloyd's*, 8.
2   Piano + Rogers Architects, 'A Design Strategy for Lloyd's', 44.
3   John Carter, 'Management Contracting', *The Architects' Journal* 156, no. 50 (1972), 1371.
4   For the following historical development of the general contractor approach and George A. Fuller, cf. Sarah Wermiel, 'Norcross, Fuller and the Rise of the General Contractor in the United States in the Nineteenth Century', in Malcom Dunkeld, ed., *Proceedings of the Second International Congress on Construction History*, vol. 3 (Exeter: Construction History Society; Short Run Press, 2006), 3297–3313.
5   Cf. Wermiel, 'Norcross, Fuller', 3306.
6   Cf. Peter Cooper, *Building Relationships: The History of Bovis* (London: Cassell & Co, 2000), 51.
7   Cf. Carter, 'Management Contracting', 1371.
8   Shamil G. Naoum and David Langford, 'Management Contracting: The Client's View', *Journal of Construction Engineering and Management* 113, no. 3 (1987), 373.
9   Cf. Cooper, *Building Relationships*, 131, 137.
10 Naoum and Langford, 'Management Contracting', 384.
11 'Design Team Meeting Minutes', Archive RSHP, 148.
12 'Design Team Memos/Information', Archive RSHP, London, 262.
13 Hannay, 'Two Politics of Patronage', 55.
14 'Coordination Meeting Minutes', Archive RSHP, 213.
15 'Team Review of Mock-Ups, Meeting Minutes', 1980–1983, Archive Arup, London, 2–8.
16 'Team Review of Mock-Ups, Meeting Minutes', 3.
17 'Team Review of Mock-Ups, Meeting Minutes', 4.
18 'Team Review of Mock-Ups, Meeting Minutes', 2.

6. Looking for Answers

It stimulates the discussion; it's a trigger process; the mock-up isn't necessarily the answer – it's a way to the answer.[1]

Mike Davies

The launch of an extensive mock-up programme for the Lloyd's Building was one of the first measures taken by the new constellation of the design team with Bovis as the management contractor. The programme provided technical and constructive solutions to the architectural concepts and technical system promised in the design, and it also reduced the risks of their implementation.

The mock-up programme ran at a workshop site in Fulham until the end of 1982 and was adapted and expanded several times over two years. At twenty-five 'team review of mock-up meetings',[2] representatives from Richard Rogers + Partners (RRP), Ove Arup & Partners, MDA and Bovis discussed the ongoing progress, findings and further measures. During these meetings, it became apparent that the questions formulated in the

6.01 The finished Mock-Up One on the Bovis factory yard in Fulham [1982?]

programme specification could not be answered without further investigations and additional mock-ups. This was particularly true of Mock-Up One, which provided the impetus for a whole series of further investigations and clarifications. These investigations were primarily directed to the processes of construction, manufacturing or building part operation and included questions such as how the beam grid could be shuttered, the facade system assembled, the structured glass embossed, the envelope cavity ventilated and the interior ventilated and illuminated. Different findings from the various mock-ups were combined to iteratively find a solution ready for construction and were finally implemented in Mock-Up One (6.01).

As the following reconstruction of the programme[3] based on these selected mock-ups shows, the mock-up programme shifted the focus of the design team away from conceptual and systemic issues to constructive and technical issues of the actual building components. In the end, the mock-up programme provided not only answers but also unexpected insights, helping foster a sense of mutual trust among all collaborators and developing buildable constructions.

Shuttering the Beam Grid

The beam grid for the Lloyd's Building had to be legible as a uniform construction assembled of individual beams to support the concept of a seemingly endless, homogeneous space. This could not be achieved with the prevailing construction method. Generally, beam grids are made up of hollow elements positioned on the falsework and removed from below after the concrete has hardened. To be able to retract such coffers without them getting stuck, they are made conical, thus resulting in conical beams. The joints of coffer elements are also visible on the beam soffit as longitudinal joints. Both the conical shape and the joints destroy the visual integrity of a beam and instead accentuate the bay of the beam grid. This method therefore was not an option for the Lloyd's beam grid; instead, a formwork had to be found which articulated the beams by making their sides parallel, the edges sharp and the soffits free of longitudinal joints.

RRP's intention to leave the concrete structure of the beam grid visible created concern from Lloyd's:

> When we proposed an exposed in situ concrete structure to the client, they were taken aback and asked Richard and me to show them examples of what we had in mind in England. We said there were none, and there were none in Europe, we'd have to go to the States.[4]

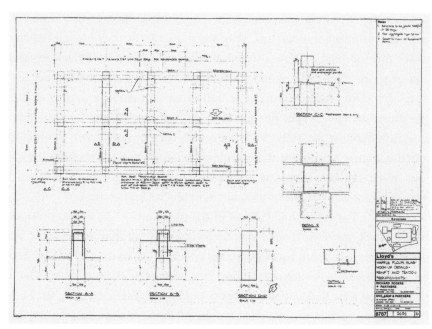

6.02 Working drawing of the first structural mock-up, Ove Arup & Partners, March 1981

Since the construction would remain visible, the workmanship, surface and colour of the concrete would also need to meet the highest requirements. At the end of April 1981, Young, together with Blackmore from Lloyd's, client representative John Bathgate and Bovis director Brian Pettifier, travelled to the United States for two weeks to inspect exposed concrete in buildings by I.M. Pei and Louis Kahn.

The specifications of the mock-up programme included the steps to evaluate a formwork system that would meet the high demands on the beam grid's construction and its concrete quality. It was planned that Bovis propose various formwork systems for casting 3.6-by-3.6-metre sections of the beam grid based on requirements from Ove Arup & Partners and RRP. These mock-ups were to be made four metres above the ground and include a construction joint. In this way, not only the quality of the final product could be evaluated but also the working processes of construction. In the preparation of this first structural mock-up for evaluating the formwork system, a plywood formwork and combinations of different systems in one mock-up were considered. Finally, it was decided to produce the structural mock-up with formwork moulds made of glass-fibre reinforced plastic from the company Barnes using two-by-three fields. Since the beam grid did not yet have its final shape, the different beams still had different heights, making the formwork construction more complex.

The mock-up was concreted in mid-June 1981 and then struck. As the working drawing from Ove Arup & Partners for this mock-up shows, the glass-fibre reinforced plastic elements were struck upward, causing the conical cross-section of the beam to taper toward the top (rather than the bottom, as in the commonly used method where the elements are struck downward) (6.02). This prevented accentuation of the bay of the beam grid. Furthermore, this method allowed the soffit to be formed in one piece without joints in the middle. In addition, a steel formwork from the French company Vissa was to be evaluated. It would not need to be conical because it was constructed to be folded inward so it could be struck without any risk of the coffers getting stuck when retracted. Beams concreted in this way have parallel flanks, which Ove Arup & Partners and RRP preferred to those with a trapezoidal cross-section. For cost reasons, it was decided not to construct a new mock-up but to extend the structural mock-up by two bays. Vissa's late delivery of the formwork led to a delay of about a month for these additions to the mock-up.

The structural mock-up had disappointing results. In addition to poorly formed joints, there appeared to be problems with Vissa's steel formwork. The beams that were produced did not have parallel flanks, indicating that the formwork had become deformed when the concrete was placed. The mock-up did not yet have the quality that Ove Arup & Partners and RRP were looking for in the beam grid: 'The first results were not good enough, but we learned an enormous amount, particularly about the design of the formwork joints that would give the quality of finish required, and built a second set incorporating refinements.'[5]

Due to the poor results of the first mock-up, it was decided in mid-June 1981 to produce further mock-ups using three different systems (6.03). For reasons of cost and scheduling, the mock-ups of this second series of experiments were only two bays large rather than six bays in the first mock-up. They were poured on the ground and then lifted onto a scaffold to inspect the soffit. During the preparations, the possibility of inserting adding fillets to the formwork to form grooves was to be checked (6.04, 6.05).

Around the same time, Ove Arup & Partners determined the final dimensioning of the beam grid. This second series of tests was not originally planned and required adjustments to the schedule for Mock-Up One (6.06). Within each column field, all beams would now have the same height. This would not only simplify the installation of cables and ducts but also lead to simpler formwork elements. In addition to the Vissa steel formwork already in use, new glass-fibre reinforced plastic moulds from Butcher and a

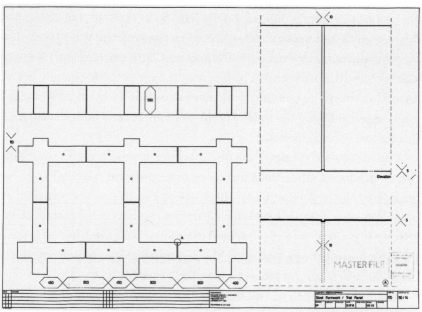

6.03 Two-bay mock-ups of different formwork systems at the Bovis work yard in Fulham, 1981

6.04 Joint pattern for Vissa's formwork system, RRP

6.05 Detailed design: joint pattern of beam grid (does not correspond with final construction), RRP, March 1982

6.06 Schedule for the two-bay mock-ups (here called 'Further Structural Mock-Ups') and their effect on the final Mock-Up One, Bovis, July 1981

400/239   Main frame
Beam markings: Isometric

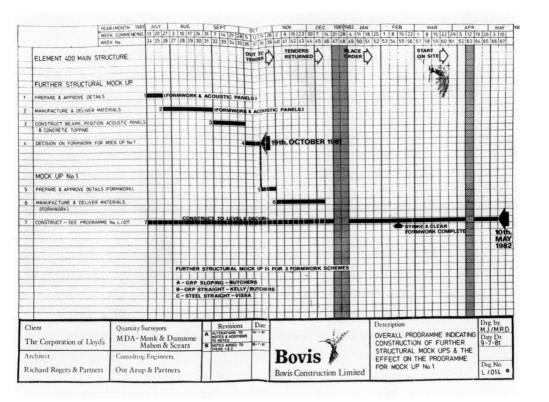

137

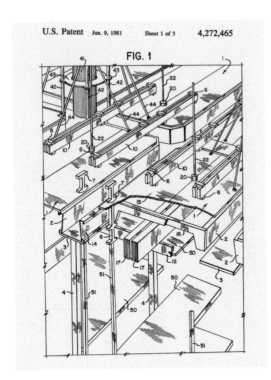

6.07 System drawing of the patented formwork system by Reginald Hough and Vincent Kelly

formwork system made of coated plywood by American concrete specialists Reginald Hough and Vincent Kelly were to be tested. Young met Hough and Kelly on a trip to the United States with representatives of Bovis and Lloyd's:

> It was during a visit to I.M. Pei's office that we met Reg Hough who was working there virtually full time as a consultant, and it was from that meeting that the idea of employing Kelly Hough as concrete consultants on Lloyd's first arose in an attempt to achieve a quality of concrete never seen before in Britain.[6]

Hough and Kelly held a patent for a formwork system composed of small elements for quickly moving the formwork from one storey to the next without lateral manoeuvring surfaces (6.07).[7] They thus had experience with formwork systems designed as reusable kits and therefore (against Bovis's will) were brought in as consultants to develop another formwork system:

> Bovis weren't happy about it [the consultancy mandate from Vincent Kelly], they felt they knew everything there was to know about concrete, but Lloyd's fortunately backed us, and the results of the success of that collaboration are plain to see.[8]

6.08 Kelly system, October 1981
a Removal of formwork
b Finished formwork
c Formwork of stub column above grid node

Kelly travelled to London several times, where he supervised the production of the plywood formwork by the company Barretts and then the production of the mock-up. Kelly's system consisted of many individual parts, so the formwork construction was time-consuming. Bovis wrote a detailed report on this second series of tests, describing the structure of the three formwork systems and listing the experience gained during manufacture.[9] Work safety, parts handling, time required, tolerances and accuracy, formwork maintenance and element storage were all considered. Main questions included if the soffit needed a work floor, if the pieces were light enough to be worn and if the parts could be joined together quickly and easily; if errors would add up or balance themselves out; if the concrete could be placed and removed easily and quickly; and if the shuttering was tight enough to prevent grout from leaking. For the formwork, questions abounded regarding whether it could be struck simply, safely and without much force; if it could be easily cleaned and reused; if it could be easily and safely stored without losing

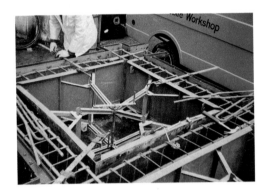 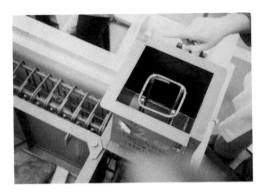

parts; if its construction could be adjusted (for example, to align the plinths); and if the reinforcement cages could be placed in the assembled formwork or if they would have to be mounted with the formwork. Special attention was paid to the quality of concrete. In the final chapter of the report, the costs of the floor slab were calculated for the respective formwork systems.

The Bovis report listed the findings without comparing and assessing the three formwork systems, as the choice of system in the tender was left to the offering company. With regard to the Kelly system, Bovis noted that the different formwork parts – especially the formwork for the stub columns – could hardly be adjusted. Bovis also feared that small parts – advantageous in making the system easily storable and transportable across storeys without a crane – would be lost and that the system would have to be constantly supplemented. The Kelly system optimally solved the sealing of the many joints, a critical point of this system, with the best concrete quality. The surfaces, unlike with the other two systems, met a high standard. Furthermore, the system was very dimensionally stable (6.08a–c).

The Vissa system was notable for its easy removal of the formwork. In addition, the formwork for the base consisted of a single part and thus could be easily adjusted on the structural node. Nevertheless, formwork construction was complex. All parts were heavy and would have to be moved by crane or by two people. The formwork would have to be resealed every time, which would be time-consuming and prone to errors. With both formwork elements, there were (as probably already with the first mock-up) problems with the folding mechanism. The internal stiffening, which ensured that the formwork was not compressed by the concrete pressure, did not fulfil its function and would have to be provisionally supported. Striking, however, was very easy with this system, but Bovis noted that the mechanism was susceptible to concrete deposits and the system would have to be constantly and thoroughly cleaned. Although the concrete surface was good, it was

6.09 Vissa system, October 1981
a Finished formwork
b Formwork of stub column above grid node

6.10 Butcher system, October 1981
a Removal of formwork
b Finished formwork
c Formwork of stub column above grid node

not of the quality of the Kelly system. With deformations averaging four centimetres, the stability of the formwork left much to be desired (6.09a–b).

The Butcher system, made of glass-fibre reinforced plastic elements, would allow the formwork to be built fastest. The big disadvantage of this system was the difficulty in striking the formwork. The form inclination of the elements was so small that they tilted during striking, not only making the process extremely time-consuming but also causing individual corners and edges to break. Unlike wood and steel, the glass-fibre reinforced plastic elements were susceptible to damage, necessitating careful inspection and repair before reuse. They were also very unstable, leading to deformations of up to twelve centimetres. The concrete quality of the surface was good according to the report by Bovis (6.10a–c).

In the cost comparison of the three systems, the Kelly system was the most expensive, followed by the Vissa system (about 17 per cent cheaper) and then the glass-fibre reinforced plastic moulds from the Butcher company (40 per cent cheaper). Regardless of the quality of the mock-ups, the process had also demonstrated the reliability of the individual suppliers – not least in terms of delivery and their commitment to the further development of the systems.

Although the Bovis report made no recommendation, from the point of view of the design team, the Kelly system was clearly preferred. Even before the second series of tests had been completed, the Kelly system had been decided upon:

> Discussion on the part that formwork drawings play in the 400 [substructure] tender documentation. Agreed that the Kelly drawings would be available as background information. In the documentation we do not say that Kelly's method is the only method but, this is one way of going about it.[10]

The decision for the Kelly system was probably made not only because of the expected quality of the concrete but also because of the high degree of control of the formwork pattern that was possible with this system – for example, rebates and grooves in the concrete surface could be created relatively easily with strips.

Mock-Up One was the last in a series of mock-ups and brought together all the knowledge gained from previous mock-ups. The floor slab of Mock-Up One was three-by-four fields large and contained a U-beam with line breakthroughs in addition to the beam grid. The construction was originally to be carried out by the subcontractor, but as this was not yet organised, Bovis shouldered the work. The formwork was to be executed with the Kelly system. Since Barretts, which had manufactured the elements for the two-bay mock-up, required too long a lead time to produce new elements, the company Samuel Elliot & Sons was commissioned as the new subcontractor. In addition to improvements to the formwork of the beam grid, the connections or construction joints on the U-beams, the size and position of the openings in the U-beam and the position of inserts for the facade were determined. The floor slab was concreted in two work steps to check the control of construction joints (6.11, 6.12).

In early December 1981, the substructure package was put out to tender and the contract awarded to Gleeson in February 1982. Gleeson offered its services based on the Kelly system, which it developed into a sophisticated kit together with RRP and Bovis after the contract was awarded (6.13, 6.14a–f): 'Gleeson, the subcontractor who won the contract to produce the concrete

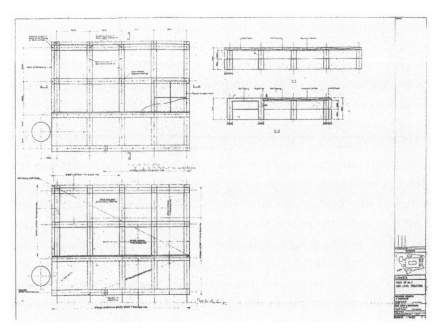

6.11 Mock-Up One after completion of the beam grid. The glazing system from the structural mock-up was built in spring 1982.

6.12 Plan for beam grid of Mock-Up One, Ove Arup & Partners, November 1981

6.13 Complete kit for the Gleeson formwork system, dismantled into individual parts

frame also gets a lot of credit for the success, and for their role in working with the team in developing the formwork system for the floors.'[11]

The load-bearing parts of the system were made of steel profiles, with only the parts in contact with concrete cast in coated plywood (6.15a). This made the system slimmer and lighter and improved handling. A key detail was the sealing of the joint between the beam and the beam grid node: a neoprene gasket was embedded in the seam of a steel plate folded multiple times and attached to the front of the plywood formwork (6.15b). The horizontal form-work panel for the beams soffit rested on the formwork for the beam grid node (6.15c); for the vertical beam sides, posts made of steel angles served as a stop (6.15d). In the cast concrete, this joint was visible as a groove. A steel profile suspended between the posts secured the formwork and simultan-eously absorbed the formwork pressure (6.15e). Ties between the formwork were thus unnecessary, so the sides of the beam could be made without any tie points. To also control the surface on the beam soffit, special reinforce-ment spacers made of threaded sleeves were developed that at the same time served as fixing points for internal partitions.[12]

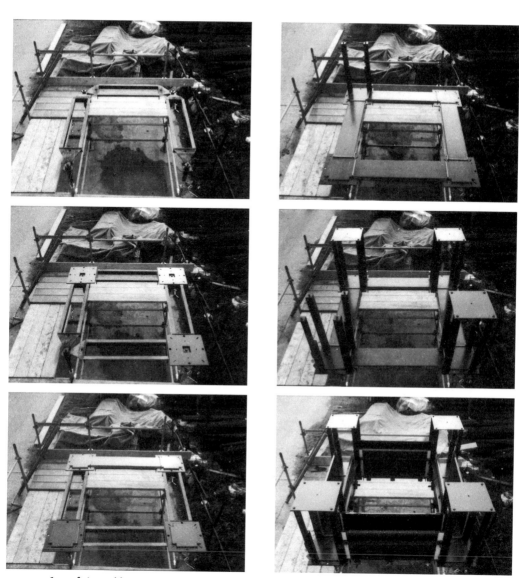

6.14a–f Assembly sequence of Gleeson formwork, 1982

The four posts in the corners of the section not only absorbed the horizontal forces of the fresh concrete; they also supported the stub columns at the beam grid nodes, which were no longer made of in-situ concrete (as in the mock-ups) but rather cast as prefabricated parts with the rest of the construction. The precast element hung from a mounting plate attached to the four steel posts (6.15f), enabling the bases to be adjusted and aligning independently of the rest of the formwork. After the concrete hardened, the mounting plate could be removed. The lost formwork for the floor plate was attached to the threaded sleeve of the precast element.

145

The kit developed by Gleeson proved very successful for the logistics on the construction site (7.04a–7.04h). Because the formwork could be disassembled into individual parts and moved manually through the beam grid to the next floor, the construction cranes were freed to be used for other purposes. This was essential for maintaining the tight schedule.[13] In addition, the visual quality of the beam grid was also excellent:

> Everyone who knows anything about concrete agrees that this is work of the highest quality. There has been very little repair work necessary despite literally miles of sharp arris. The in-situ concrete was simply washed down to remove water marks, and the precast was lightly sand-blasted. The painstaking research and testing procedure has paid dividends and much credit is due to the subcontractor, Gleeson's.[14]

Assembling the Facade System

For the scheme design, RRP designed the facade for the Lloyd's Building as a system of individual joined aluminium profiles, following the tradition of Ludwig Mies van der Rohe's facades. RRP included an I-beam mullion on the axes of the beam grid. To minimize risks during facade construction, problems regarding the penetration detail of the ceiling support, the deflection of the mullions under horizontal load, the assembly sequence of the facade and the tolerance compensation for assembly and movement deviations had to be solved.

In the autumn of 1980, RRP visited the Gartner factory in Gundelfingen, Germany, known for its experience with ventilated facades. At the end of October 1980, the Gartner company (which later received the order for the facade and other work packages such as the steel structure of the atrium, the escape stairs and the cladding of the sanitary blocks) drew the first plans for the facade system. In contrast to the scheme design, where the facade was

6.15 Formwork assembly, 1982
a Formwork element for the soffit of the beam grid node. Next to it are four steel posts, which serve as a stopper for the lateral formwork elements.
b Folded steel plate with an embedded neoprene gasket at the joint to ensure tight connections of the formwork elements. The folded steel plate creates a groove in the finished concrete that will refer to the functioning of the formwork.
c Formwork of the node and beam soffit. The raised, folded steel plate is clearly visible in the joint of the two elements.
d The four posts fixed with wedges
e Steel profiles mounted between the posts to absorb the concrete pressure
f Mounting plate to hang the precast stub columns into the formwork

divided into three horizontal elements (4.37a), the horizontal division was increased to four. Apart from that revision, the drawings largely followed RRP's solution of a mullion-transom system, with the mullion profile serving as a stop for the insulating glazing. The cavity between the inner and outer layer was extended to form an H-beam, and it simultaneously functioned both as a pressure bar for the outer glazing and as a fixing for the inner glazing (6.16a).

In December, Gartner proposed an alternative facade system with split mullions to RRP: prefabricated facade panels would be installed by pushing one into the other laterally, with joints absorbing horizontal movements. Gartner had already used this novel system in several projects to the great satisfaction of clients and general contractors since the high degree of prefabrication minimised the installation time. The detail of horizontal joint of the facade was subsequently revised in several variants (6.16b). Gartner also clarified how the load-bearing capacity of the mullions would absorb horizontal wind forces. Especially on the ground floor (with a ceiling height of nine metres), the load-bearing capacity of the normal profile was insufficient and had to be reinforced.

In May 1981, RRP sent Chamebel and Gartner, the two facade companies with whom they were in contact, the current state of the design for examination. The revised details Gartner returned in early June were presumably the basis of the mock-up of the facade that Gartner offered for twenty-three thousand British pounds and which RRP commissioned the same month (6.16b). The mock-up was five fields large and included the corner detail and a tilting window. It was to be mounted on a steel frame by itself and later integrated into Mock-Up One (6.18a–e). Another mock-up of a wooden facade element was to be produced in London in June to help RRP determine the vertical division of the facade, the position of the tilting window and the design of the mullion profile.

The Gartner mock-up arrived in London in mid-August but was not mounted on the steel frame as planned; rather, it was mounted on the mock-up of the beam grid so that its profiles and glass could be assessed under natural conditions. The mock-up was also closed at the sides and top with a construction of chipboard and plasterboard to create a space and protect the facade (6.19a–b). Except for the mullion profiles, it was to be composed of bent steel plates and standard profiles instead of extruded profiles (6.16c, 6.18a). The arrangement layout and dimensions of the facade system were, with the exception of minor deviations, identical to the revised design from the beginning of July. Gartner did not glaze the mock-up with the intended structured glass (which had not yet been completed at that time) but with

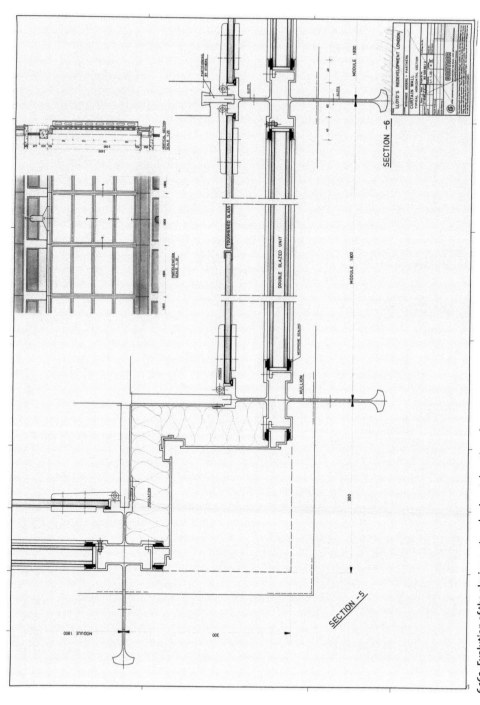

6.16a Evolution of the glazing system, horizontal section of corner
Drawings for acquisition, 27 October 1980

149

6.16b Glazing system mock-up, shop drawings, 1981
First executed version of the inner openable glass pane with glass fittings, 14 July

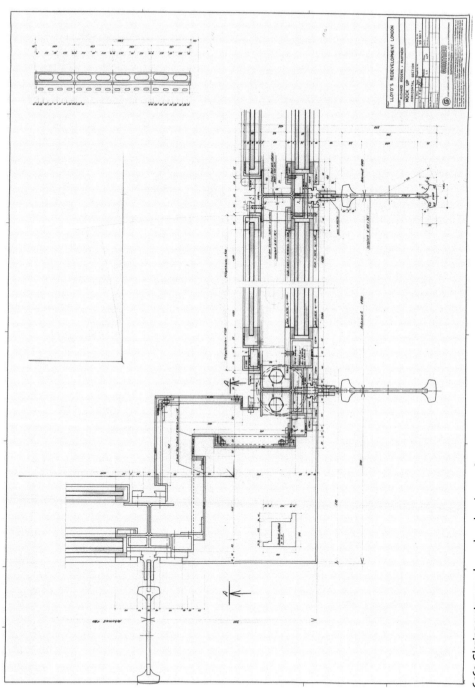

6.16c Glazing system mock-up, shop drawings, 1981
Mounting frame for the glazing system mock-up, 23 July

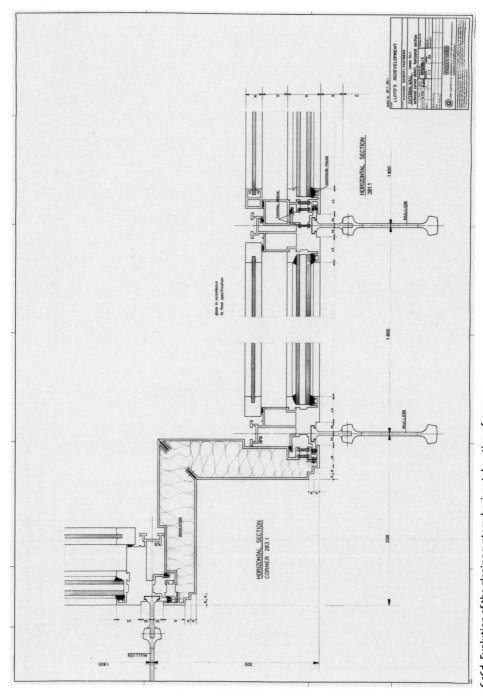

6.16d Evolution of the glazing system, horizontal section of corner
Drawing for the offer, 16 November 1981

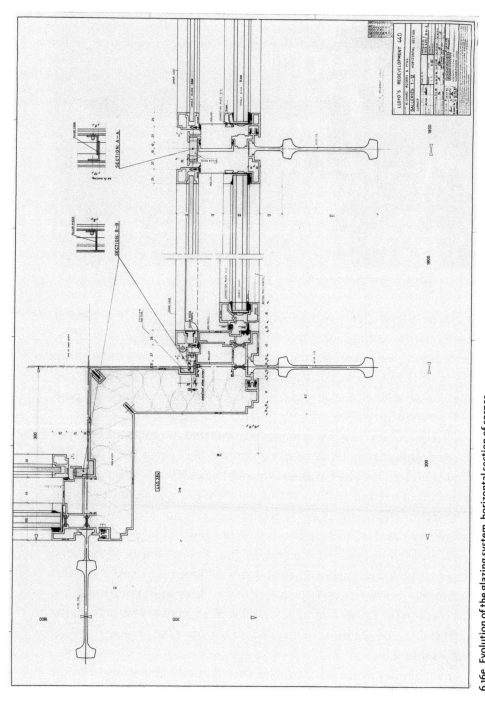

6.16e Evolution of the glazing system, horizontal section of corner
Shop drawings, 26 April 1982

6.17 Cross section of glazing system [1982?]

commercially available structured glass (6.20a).[15] On this mock-up, different low-emissivity coatings for sun control were tested and the sections of the outer glazing were fixed, but the planned tilting window was still missing. The inner facade of a section consisted of three pivoting windows arranged one above the other, whose glass side hinges were fixed through the glass with point fixings (6.18b).

The assembly of the facade mock-up revealed some problems of the produced profile system. While erecting it, three glass panes from the inner glazing broke due to bad workmanship and unsuitable glass fittings. As a result, Gartner reworked the construction of the inner frame and produced new elements for the mock-up. The revised construction of the inner facade system consisted of a single circumferential glass frame attached to the mullions with hinges (6.18d). Because the glass was cemented into the frame, the construction was approximately twenty millimetres deeper. There was no internal facade system at the height of the tilting window, so the gap to the space in the facade had to be closed with an additional profile. At the same time as the new inner frame, Gartner also drew and produced a tilting window (6.18e).

In mid-November, 1981, Gartner delivered a new complete set of facade plans (6.16d). Individual details were marked with item numbers, indicating that these plans were most likely part of Gartner's offer for the facade tender package. Gartner proposed an alternative construction of the mullions that

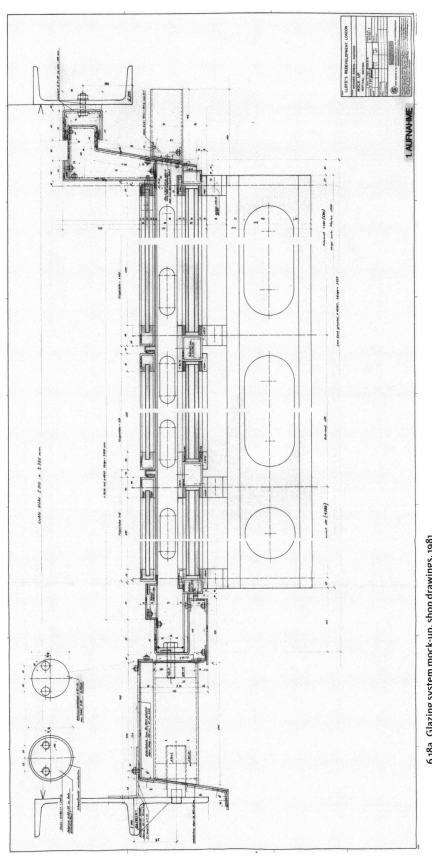

6.18a Glazing system mock-up, shop drawings, 1981
Vertical section, 7 July

6.18b Glazing system mock-up, shop drawings, 1981
First executed version of the inner openable glass pane with glass fittings, 14 July

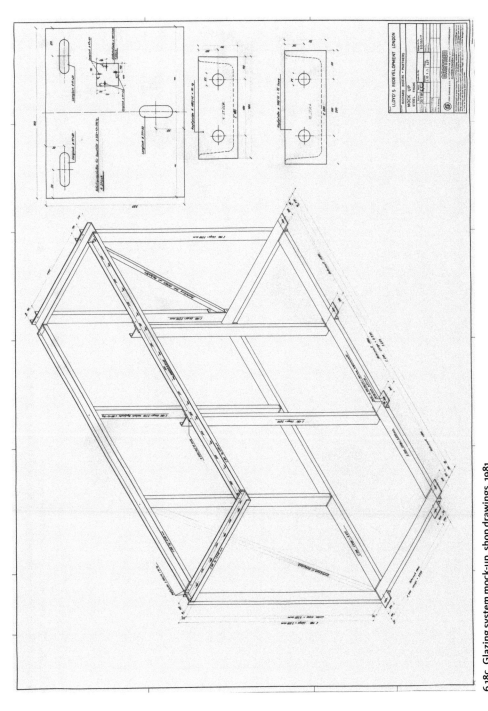

6.18c Glazing system mock-up, shop drawings, 1981
Mounting frame for the glazing system mock-up, 23 July

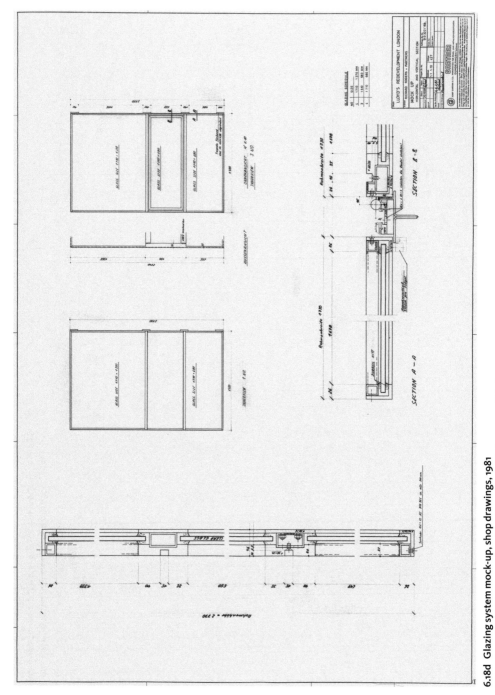

6.18d Glazing system mock-up, shop drawings, 1981
Second version of the inner openable glass pane with frame, 20 October

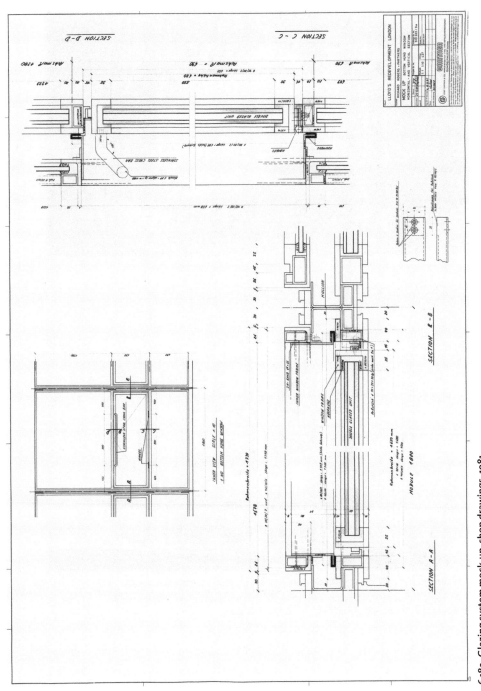

6.18e Glazing system mock-up, shop drawings, 1981
Details of the tilting window, 27 October

6.19 Mock-up of the glazing system positioned on the raised structural mock-up
a At night with spotlights to check the effect of the structured glass, October 1981
b Reworked with a clear glazed field in the upper position

deviated from tender drawings by RRP. The mullion was constructed using two hollow profiles (each one pushed into the other), and it was considerably wider than the previous variants where the mullion was made of a six-millimetre bar. Gartner's alternative resulted in improved stability, allowing production of the facade as individual elements. This also offered an

6.20a Mock-up of the glazing system, glazed with standard structured glass. Strip windows are mounted in all sections at seat height, October 1981.

6.20b Reworked mock-up of the glazing system with structured glass from Vegla's test production. A strip window has been moved to eye-level when standing, spring 1982

alternative for how to guide the exhaust air of the ventilated cavity through the hollow profile.[16]

In January 1982, a few weeks after being awarded the contract to manufacture the facade, Gartner installed the new elements of the internal facade. While the new inner frames and the tilting window were being installed in the mock-up, RRP requested that a field be converted so that the clear glazed portion was in the upper position. Simultaneously, the mock-up was completely glazed with structured glass from a test production by Vegla (6.19b, 6.20b, 6.21).[17] Subsequently, it was detected that the external facade system had leaks, presumably due to the temporary construction. Nevertheless, the corresponding detail was revised to adjust it when reinstalled in Mock-Up One. This point was given special attention in the ordered weathering tests, which Gartner carried out during the fabrication planning (6.22, 6.23). In addition to these weathering tests, Gartner also performed load tests of the mullion profile for the ground floor as part of the fabrication planning (6.24).

At the end of June 1982, the mock-up of the facade was removed from the structural mock-up and installed in Mock-Up One (6.11). Finally, at the

beginning of August, the clear glazed field was reattached at the lower position and the mock-up was glazed with new structured glass from Vegla (6.25). During the installation of the facade mock-up in Mock-Up One, Gartner gained additional experience regarding the accuracy of the substructure to be expected during the real construction. This raised awareness of possible complications on the construction site already during the fabrication planning, so Gartner developed a special fastening to accommodate for deviations of the substructure's dimensions and also for later movements of the structure (7.06a). This fastening was designed of a cast aluminium part with an adjustable, threaded cylinder that connected the structure with the facade system via two hinge joints (7.06c, 7.06e, 7.07a–b).

The work on the facade mock-up revealed several problems of the original facade system and helped to continuously develop and optimise a system that not only could resist wind and weather but also overcame the limitation of a mullion-transom system (6.16e, 6.17): the largest element of the final facade system was not the single profile but the whole window. These components were manufactured at Gartner's factory in Germany, loaded into a truck in their sequence of assembly and delivered from Gundelfingen to London, where they could be joined one after the other in a smooth construction process.

Embossing the Structured Glass

The optical and visual properties of structured glass for the glazing of the Lloyd's Building are decisive to the atmospheric qualities of the interior of the building. The desired sparkly effect was not the only criterion for developing the structured glass. Its manufacturing process and production conditions were equally critical for the final product and had to be clarified before the construction of the building.

Production plants for structured glass, in which U-shaped cast glass (called U-glass) is also manufactured, are less common than plants for the more common float glass, which comprises 95 per cent of all flat glass produced. In the production of float glass, the molten glass flows onto a liquid

6.21 Reworked mock-up of the glazing system: inner openable glass pane with frames instead of glass fittings, spring 1982
6.22 Weather testing of the facade at Gartner in Gundelfingen with a delegation from the design team [1982?]
6.23 Weather testing of the facade: measuring system [1982?]
6.24 Load testing of the mullion for the ground floor [1982?]
6.25 Mock-Up One shortly before completion, summer 1982

tin bath and solidifies. To produce structured glass, a glass melt is instead pressed from a tank through a pair of rollers. It is then guided over several rollers, whereby the mass solidifies to form a pane (6.26). The structure engraved in the rollers is embossed into the surface of the glass pane and repeated in the direction of flow with each rotation of the roller (6.27, 6.28). Since the glass is not yet completely solidified after the first rolling and embossing process, small tolerances in the embossed structure are very difficult to achieve. Commercially available structured glass is therefore often embossed with irregular patterns, where inaccuracies are less noticeable. For the structured glass for the Lloyd's Building a manufacturer had to be found that was able to deal with fine patterns and small tolerances.

The glass manufacturer Pilkington, who had already worked with Rogers's team on several research projects,[18] was approached by RRP to cooperate in developing the structured glass for the Lloyd's Building. Although the plant was not yet adequately equipped for the development of a structured glass, Pilkington agreed and promised to establish the necessary facilities for doing trial casts of various pattern designs. In addition, the company made an optical glass specialist available to the design team to advise them on developing the sparkly effect.

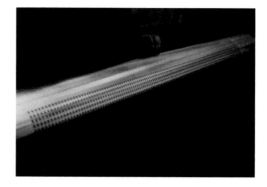

6.26 Production plant for structural glass

6.27 Roller for the large lenses: the smooth surface divides the patterned zones

6.28 Different embossing rollers to make the final roller. The fine structure is on the same side as the large lenses

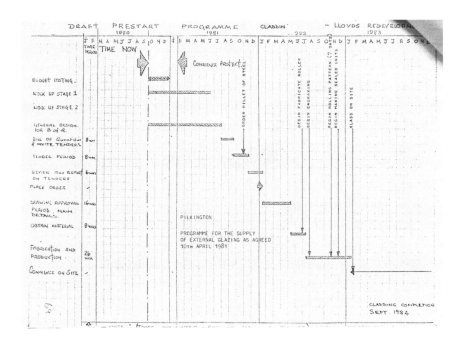

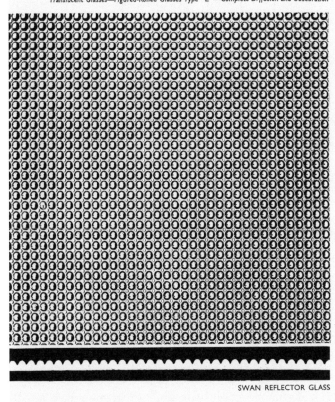

Translucent Glasses—Figured-Rolled Glasses Type ' E '—Complete Diffusion and Obscuration

SWAN REFLECTOR GLASS

6.29 Pilkington's production programme for the structured glass. The lead time to production was twelve months; seven days were planned for the production itself. Pilkington, April 1981

6.30 Chance Brothers structured glass, referred to by Stephen Le Roith in a letter to Pilkington

Because the development of the glass design made slow progress, at a meeting in February 1981 with Rogers, Rice and Lloyd's Building Commission Chair Courtenay Blackmore, Pilkington was made aware of the urgency to clarify the manufacturing of the structured glass. Pilkington agreed to examine the feasibility, deadlines and budget for producing 1.8-metre wide ornamental glass – both in its own plant and in its new German subsidiary, Flachglas AG. The lead time for engraving the roller, which Pilkington estimated at four to five months, also needed to be checked. These clarifications were delayed, however, because Pilkington's board had to decide on the costs of adapting the production plant. Finally, Pilkington stated that the delivery period for the steel blank for the roller would be nine months, resulting in a total lead time for the start of production of the glass of approximately one year from the date of ordering the blank (6.29).

At the same time, Stephen Le Roith, the newly appointed team leader of the facade design, started working on the pattern of the embossed structure. The pattern was intended not only to make the glass translucent but also to bundle the light rays so that the glass pane appeared as a sheet of light. In a letter to Pilkington, he referred to a glass by Chance Brothers from a 1937 catalogue (6.30). Combining two patterns with large and small lens profiles would create a sparkly effect of different intensities and more surface texture.

Le Roith discussed these first drafts with the specialists from Pilkington. The variations differed mainly in the arrangement of the large lenticular embossing, which was grouped in larger blocks or round motifs. One variant was still influenced by the image of a glass block wall: small lenses formed round clusters with a diameter of ten centimetres, distributed on an orthogonal grid on the pane. Since the structure on the glass was divided into horizontal blocks that had to correspond to the horizontal division of the facade, the unwinding (respectively the circumference of the roller) had to be adjusted to this dimension. Pilkington preferred an option with four blocks spread across the width of the glass, of which they cast a sample in acrylic glass. The profile of the lenses has not yet been resolved.

Although the mock-up specifications stated that RRP would develop the structure of the glass with Pilkington, RRP contacted other glass manufacturers. At a meeting between RRP and Vegla (mainly concerning technical aspects of the fire-resistant glass Contraflam), it emerged that Vegla – unlike Pilkington – already had a plant capable of producing ornamental glass with the required width of 1.8 metres and could produce samples in smaller dimensions. By May 1981, first samples were available from Pilkington and Vegla, and the company Glaverbel was asked for further samples.

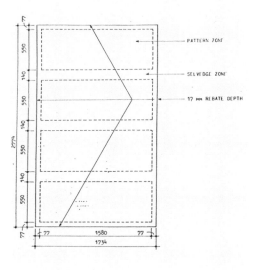
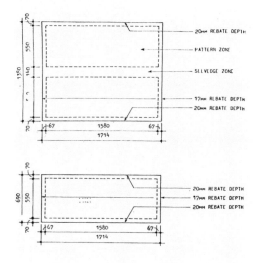

DIMENSIONS OF LOWER GROUND FLOOR PATTERN GLASS

DIMENSIONS OF TYPICAL FLOOR PATTERN GLASS

6.31 Pattern layout based on the same roller for the different glass panels, RRP, July 1981
a Glass panel for the basement with four patterned zones
b Glass panels for the ground floor and typical floors with two- respectively one-patterned zones

Meanwhile, Le Roith was evolving the dimensions and the pattern of the embossing structure. To keep manufacturing costs low, he investigated structure dimensions that would allow using the same roller to produce glass with different heights. Le Roith also developed glass with vertical pitches. The dimensions were chosen so that glass could be produced with the same roller for all facades, regardless of height. With a diameter of 218 millimetres, the roller had an unwinding of 690 millimetres. Deviations from the module dimensions were absorbed in the smooth edge zone, which was also necessary for a good edge seal (6.31a–b).

For the new pattern, Le Roith embedded large lenses with a diameter of eight millimetres that would reflect light in a finer grid made of small lenses with a diameter of one millimetre that would absorb the light and make the glass translucent (6.32). The dimension of the two grids and their relative positions remained the same in the final product. In contrast to the final glass design, the embossing was only on one side, and the lens profile of the embossing was not yet geometrically defined. Le Roith received this profile from Barry Hill, the optician of the Pilkington company, at the beginning of June 1981 (6.33).

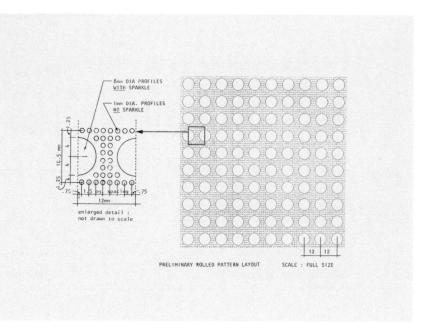

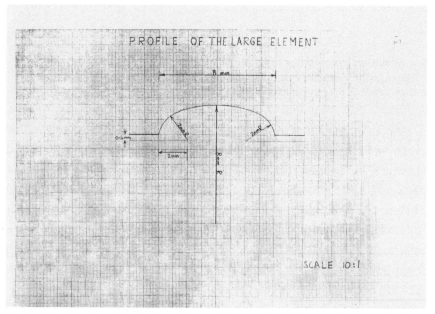

6.32, Rolled pattern layout for structured glass with large and small lenses on the same side of the glass, RRP, June 1981

6.33, Profile of the large lens to reflect light and create the sparkly effect, Pilkington, July 1981

To assess the optical effect of the new pattern, further acrylic samples were ordered from Vegla and Pilkington. These were joined with coated glass and incorporated into the mock-up of the glazing system that was mounted on the first structural mock-up of the beam grid. Because of qualitative defects, Pilkington was not able to deliver the samples: the lenses had an undesirable elliptical shape with a ratio of eight to nine. According to Pilkington, the deformation was caused by engraving the roller with a round tool, the moulette (6.28). Meanwhile, Gartner installed Vegla's samples in one of the four facade sections in early September.

The four sections of the mock-up were glazed with five differently coated glasses to check their light transmission and glare in sunlight. In addition to Vegla's acrylic samples, commercially available structured glass was also mounted to compare its sparkly effect (6.20a). At the end of October 1981, exterior lighting was installed and the Lloyd's Building commission visited the mock-up to assess the sparkle, the colour of the coated glass and the vertical position of the transparent section (6.19a).

To produce real glass samples instead of acrylic ones, Vegla proposed to use a smaller production line for the U-glass and a rolling direction horizontal to the embossing structure, with the smooth areas at the edges. The panes were only one module high and joined in the large fields of the facade with silicone. This would keep the costs of further samples low because Vegla could use a standard diameter roller in stock, which could be engraved faster, so it would not have to modify its existing facilities (6.34). Vegla estimated the cost of the sample to be half of Pilkington's price at approximately twelve thousand British pounds, with half the delivery time (two months rather than Pilkington's four for a comparable sample). After visiting Vegla at the end of

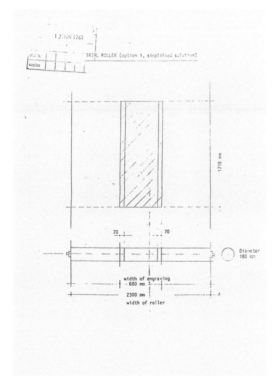

6.34 Proposal for a test roll: the diameter of the roller allows it to be used in a production line for U-glass without having to be converted. Vegla, November 1981.

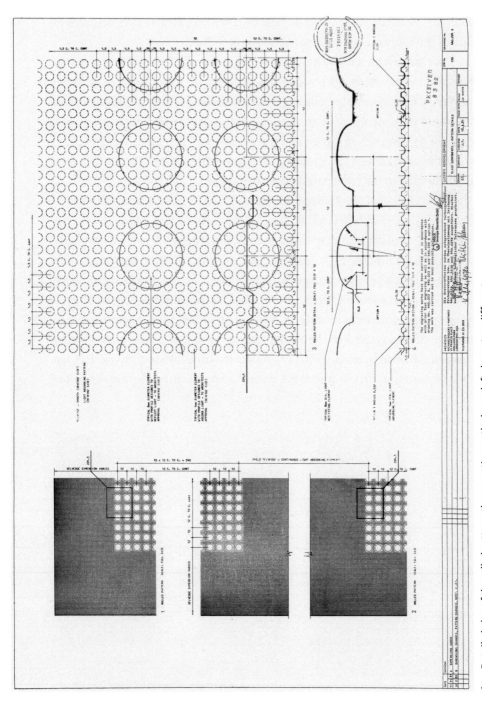

6.35 Detailed plan of the rolled pattern: the 1:1 section on the lower left shows two different options (on the left and right) for the fine structure. RRP, revision B, 22 February 1982.

6.36 Comparing the optical effect of two options of the structured glass with different types of lighting, Mock-Up One at night, 1983

a Exterior
b Interior. Clearly visible are the interferences in the fields on the left and right due to the unsuited fine structure.

6.37 Quality inspection of the structured glass. Under the large pane is a narrow pane, probably from a trial production as a comparison.

November 1981 (during the same period as the tender for the glass supply), RRP ordered appropriately produced glass panes from the company to replace the mock-up's acrylic panes. Even these sample panes still had the embossing only on one side (6.20b). At the end of 1981, Vegla was finally awarded the contract to produce the structured glass for the Lloyd's Building.

Pilkington later admitted that it probably calculated too carefully in its offer, which was around 15 per cent more expensive than Vegla's. Pilkington had wanted to have two rolls ready in case of failure or to charge for the cost of retooling the factory twice. While ordering a second roll would have delayed the start of production by three months, the cost of the conversion would have been 100,000 British pounds. Apparently, Pilkington firmly expected that the first roller would be rendered obsolete due to design changes: 'we frankly had no confidence that the first decision would be supported through to specification.' [19]

At the beginning of 1982, the glass panes supplied by Vegla were used and tested in the mock-up of the glazing system. Le Roith then drew the final revision of the embossing in which the two patterns – the lenses and fine structure – were placed on opposite sides of the glass. There were also two options for the fine structure with different heights (6.35). Vegla supplied new sample panes for both options in mid-1982 for Mock-Up One, which was already built. A comparison of the sample panes in Mock-Up One showed that undesired interference (the moiré effect) occurred with one of the two fine structures. This option was then excluded and the specification of the glass pane could be finally defined (6.36a–b).[20] All in all, Vegla invested significant time and energy to improve its facilities (6.26, 6.37). In particular, the drives of the various rollers were electrically coordinated with each other to ensure that unhardened glass would not be stretched and that there would be no deviations from the defined pattern geometry.[21]

Ventilating the Facade Cavity

For the ventilated facade cavity to optimally fulfil its purpose as an important element of the climatic concept, air would need to flow through the façade as evenly as possible without creating turbulence. Such unwanted disturbance of the airflow would lead to different surface temperatures and condensation on the glass panes and generate distracting noise. To technically implement the ventilated facade cavity, it was therefore necessary to find a way to guide the air around the openable window and to develop details for optimum airflow, which included finding the ideal shape and arrangement of the inflow and air intake opening.

A design sketch by Young shows the first approaches to solving the airflow in the facade cavity. In his sketch, he reduced the width of the openable window to one half of a facade section. This solved the problem of detouring the airflow, but Young was dissatisfied with the visual expression (4.36). RRP's first facade details in the scheme design phase show a mullion profile whose bars were perforated over the entire height of the facade by milled slots (4.37b). The two transoms of the outer and inner facade did not extend into the facade cavity, so the air could flow vertically in the sections without openable windows. In facade sections with openable windows, the air could flow around it by escaping via the lateral slits in the bars of the mullion into the adjacent sections. From there, it could flow back into the section below the openable window. This solution for airflow was pursued in Gartner's first drawings and implemented in mock-up of the glazing system that the company erected in London in August 1981 (6.16a, 6.16c).

The Gartner variant for the facade system, which was part of the company's offer, included – in addition to alternative profiles – a new approach for guiding the airflow through the cavity (6.38). Instead of directing the air above the tilting window into the adjacent facade sections, it would be guided through a lateral slot in the hollow profile to flow into the lower transom, thus becoming horizontally distributed before finally flowing through a perforation into the section below the tilting window. This would allow the areas

6.38 Drawings for the offer with a proposition for a new approach how to distribute the exhausted air in the cavity, Gartner, November 1981

directly under the bottom of the tilting window to be better ventilated than with the previous solution. The profiles were designed in such a way that they always direct air to the outer pane and along the surface in a laminar manner. If the air entered the cavity unguided, this would lead to unwanted turbulence.

In the second half of 1982, Gartner (on behalf of Ove Arup & Partners) investigated the proposed airflow. For this purpose, a mock-up was built based on the existing fabrication design already tested in Gartner's test facility in Gundelfingen (6.39), with arrangements and test findings recorded in a report.[22] This mock-up consisted of three facade sections with a tilting window in the middle section. A climate chamber was attached to the outside front in which the temperature could be reduced to −1.5 degrees Celsius. The temperature on the inside front was controlled by the test room's air

6.39 Mock-up for the air-flow tests at the Gartner company, June 1982

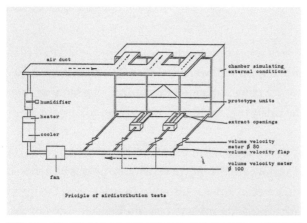

air duct
chamber simulating external conditions
humidifier
heater
cooler
prototype units
extract openings
volume velocity meter ∅ 80
volume velocity flap
volume velocity meter ∅ 100
fan

Priciple of airdistribution tests

6.40 Experimental arrangement for airflow tests, Gartner, June 1982
6.41 Mock-up for air flow tests, Gartner, June 1982

conditioning system. For the various tests, another air conditioning unit blew air from above, through the head transom and into the three facade sections. The air was then directed through the cavity, sucked out at the transom at the bottom and fed back into the air conditioning unit. This system allowed the humidity, temperature and speed of the supplied air to be controlled and varied (6.40, 6.41).

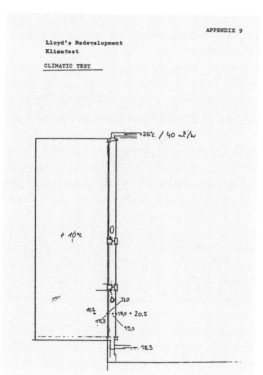

Lloyd's Redevelopment
Klimatest

CLIMATIC TEST

6.42 Example of measurement
results from the airflow tests with
different velocities and temperatures, Gartner, June 1982

To investigate the different variants of airflow, slots were milled in the profiles that could be opened or closed. Except for a profile in one facade section (which had a continuous slot of 750 by 50 millimetres), the head transoms were perforated with sixty-five holes with a diameter of fifteen millimetres each. The mullions were fitted with eight slots on the sides. All transoms of the inner glazing were formed with guides that directed the air against the outer pane. The position, number and size of the connection pieces for extracting the air at the lower transom could be varied. Smoke was used to make the air distribution and airflow visible for evaluation. Temperature measurements at various points revealed the efficiency of the system (6.42). Ultimately, the best results were achieved through perforated outlet openings in the upper transom and two air extract openings per facade section at the bottom transom. The variant with lateral inflow via the slots in the mullions clearly showed poorer results.

Guiding air through the lateral slits proved not to be a solution for the flow around the tilting window. Even with low air velocities, the results did not fulfil the requirements. Acceptable results could only be achieved by directing the air through holes into the upper transom, then into the mullions and finally into the lower transom. From there it flowed through the regularly distributed perforations into the lower section below the tilting window. By further developing Gartner's variant, the point at which the air

6.43 Shop drawing: the air holes in the mullion are added in revision G on 13 December 1982, Gartner 1982–1983.

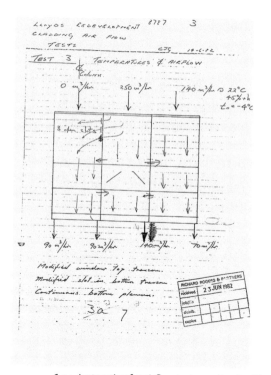

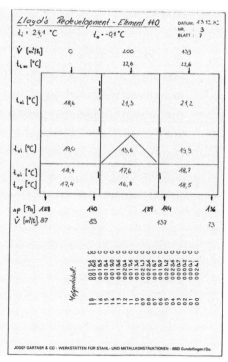

6.44 Instruction for airflow test no. 3 for checking the air distribution in the window element behind the columns. In this test, the air is introduced via three lateral slots. Ove Arup & Partners, June 1982

6.45 Measurement results for airflow test no. 3, Gartner, June 1982

was deflected (and where turbulence occurred) was moved into the transom profile (6.43). This method of air distribution allowed for the humidity of the exhausted air to rise to around 45 per cent. Beyond that value, the ventilation of the cavity would reach its limits and condensation would occur on the outer glazing panes.

In 1982, further measurements were carried out, focussing on the special condition of the facade section behind the column where the bracket penetrated the facade.[23] There, the element could not be ventilated from above (as is the case with the standard field) via the so-called fish duct: an air duct in the form of a fish tail. Instead, a solution had to be found in which the air could be drawn in from the adjacent section via slits in the posts. The air volume in this adjacent section had to be increased accordingly. The tests were intended to determine the optimum number and position of the slits, the lower suction nozzles and the air volumes per section. As in the first test series, it had to be ensured that no noise would be generated by the higher air speeds. Temperatures and pressure differences in the various sections were also measured in these tests to again assess the quality of the air distribution (6.44, 6.45).

179

Interior Ventilation

The novel air conditioning system for the Lloyd's Building, in addition to the design and construction of the exhaust air facade, raised questions of how the interior could be supplied with air without creating disturbing draughts. For this purpose, low-turbulence displacement air outlets for the floor and displacement air nozzles for the underwriters' boxes had to be developed. The Building Services Research and Information Association, a testing and research organisation, was commissioned to test the floor-to-ceiling airflow

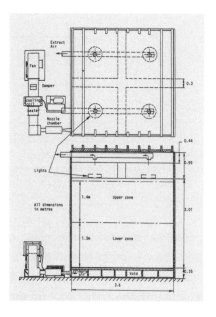

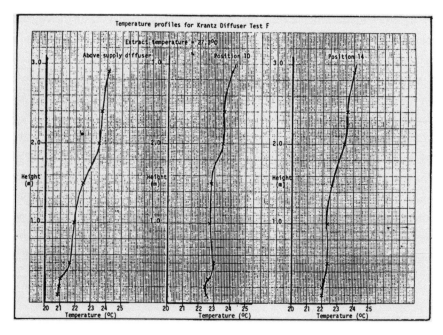

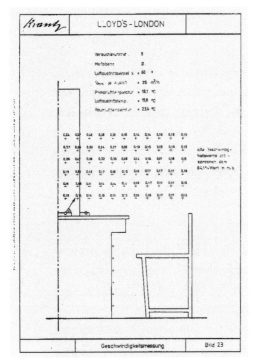 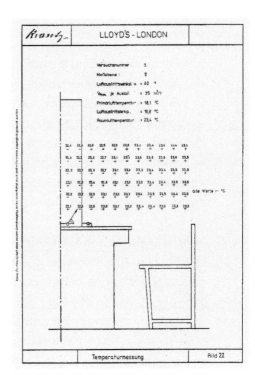

6.46 Testing of the air distribution system at the Building Services Research and Information Association

a Floor plan and section of the test room
b Test room from outside
c Measurement report of the temperature gradient for the Krantz company's twist diffuser

6.47 Test report of nozzles for the boxes, 1981

a Measurements of air velocities
b Measurements of air temperatures

system. To do so, the association built a mock-up of a typical office room with two-by-two bays of the beam grid (6.46a). To model the airflow for this mock-up, only the shape of the room and its dimensions had to correspond to the planned building. The materialisation did not have to be considered. As a result, this mock-up was built from a wooden construction closed on all sides with a raised floor and light fixtures connected to the exhaust air (6.46b). Two different air outlets were tested – a floor twist diffuser from Krantz, developed especially for the project, and a conventional linear ventilation grille – to determine the temperature gradient and the flow velocities in relation to the supply air for both diffusers (6.46c). Since the closed test room of the mock-up had heat flow paths that did not exist in the planned building, a mathematical model (validated by the test results) had to be created to extrapolate the measurements for the real building. It showed that a room temperature of 22 to 23 degrees Celsius could be achieved with the Krantz diffusers. Smoke tests confirmed that they mixed supply and room

181

air well without causing disturbing draughts.[24] The developed apparatuses and devices of this mock-up were later integrated in Mock-Up One (5.08).

While the Building Services Research and Information Association was testing the floor outlets, Krantz checked the effects of the nozzles to be integrated into the underwriters' boxes. Franc Sodec, Krantz's research manager, tested air velocity and temperature by using a prototype. The heat that would be created by people sitting at the boxes was simulated with heating mats that were placed on the benches (6.47a–b).[25]

Interior Lighting and Sprinkler System

As early as in the outline proposal, the design team proposed to combine luminaire and sprinkler fittings into a single element. For this element the design team had to develop a novel luminaire fitted with a sprinkler head and optimise the energy efficiency of the lighting and the spraying behaviour of the sprinkler head. Ove Arup & Partners began conducting measurements on the lighting in 1979 (6.48). The first prototypes of the luminaire for Mock-Up One were made by Courtney Pope Lighting in October 1981 (6.49). For the further development of the luminaire, RRP started working together with the lighting designer Friedrich Wagner from Vienna in 1983. In his small workshop, Wagner developed prototypes with reflectors made of a slightly diffuse aluminium (6.50). In parallel, sprinkler system tests were carried out to determine the effect of the reflector of the luminaire on the spraying behaviour of the sprinkler head (6.51). It had to be ensured that the bowl of the reflector did not concentrate the spray mist in an undesirable way that would result in an uneven spraying of the room. A grid of a four-by-six bay was constructed out of plywood to collect the sprayed water and to check its distribution.

After the tender of the luminaire, the development of the prototype was continued with the awarded manufacturer, Siemens. Prototypes of coloured variants (yellow, blue and violet plus striped patterns) were investigated in addition to black, white, grey and silver (6.52, 6.53a–b). The inspection of these coloured prototypes was made on the construction site rather than in Mock-Up One. The last lighting sampling took place in Mock-Up One in November 1984. It was ultimately decided to make the luminaires completely black, with rims added to fill the corners of the beam grid coffer.[26]

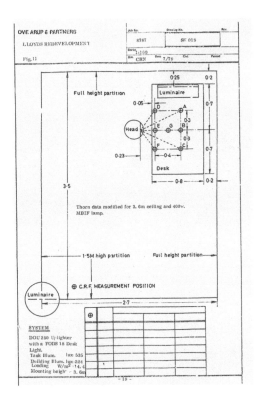

6.48 Lighting measurement, Ove Arup & Partners, July 1979

6.49 Fully equipped Mock-Up One, probably for the visit of the Special Redevelopment Committee on 19 December 1984

6.50 Luminaire prototypes
6.51 Testing the spray behaviour of the sprinkler heads integrated in luminaires, June 1982

6.52 Sketch for a luminaire with stripes, RRP, June 1984
6.53a–b Luminaire prototypes with different colours, August 1984

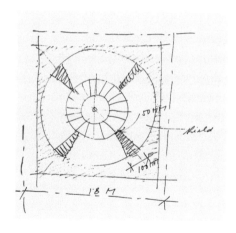

The Success of the Mock-Up Programme

In retrospect, the success of the mock-up programme is undisputed among the planners and the owners of the Lloyd's Building. John Thornton of Ove Arup & Partners asserted that 'the experience gained from the trials has been invaluable'.[27] John Smith of Bovis stated that 'some of the lessons learned in the trial runs have avoided serious problems at the site'.[28] Courtenay Blackmore of Lloyd's gave a client perspective that 'only with full-sized mock-ups can a client understand what a complex building design is all about'.[29] John Young of RRP summarised the benefits of the successful mock-up programme in four points:

> They [the mock-ups] enable the Client to see what he's getting two or three years before it appears on construction site. It quickly informs him and the designer as a means towards reaching decisions. It enables us to start an early dialogue with the District Surveyor, the Fire Brigade and other Statutory Bodies. ... The ability to agree details away from construction site is vital.
>
> It enables us to check how design decisions affect other aspects of performance such as cladding, operating and energy costs and involves the Client's own premises department.
>
> It takes the learning curve of building away from the site, so that by the time the contractor is on site, each element of the design is a tested and proven system.[30]

The reconstructed development process of the structured glass reveals this development of construction knowledge by using mock-ups rather than the building site as a place of experimentation.[31] While the investigations shifted from the arrangement of the structure to the exact geometric definition and optical calculation of the lens, known questions became more precise and new questions arose. Using mock-ups enabled the team to evolve the idea of the final product while solving its technical fabrication through repeated checks and adaptations. Moving from samples made of acrylic glass to samples made under real production conditions was necessary to identify and solve problems that were not previously detected. An example of this was the problematic moiré effect, which occurred unexpectedly with one of the fine structures and caused the light to scatter undesirably and irregularly.

Additionally, the mock-up programme forced planners to consult with various specialists to develop solutions for production. Although Vegla was ultimately awarded the contract to manufacture the structured glass,

Pilkington was also heavily involved in its development. This simultaneous collaboration with several companies brought insights that were not related to the product, as Le Roith explained: 'We worked with two companies: Vegla and Pilkington. During the process ... we had the opportunity to assess the capability of the company and their willingness to complete the job.' [32] The commitment that Vegla showed by reducing the tolerances of its production lines through innovative measures, or by looking for solutions to produce prototypes of the structured glass on an adapted plant, paid off. Not only was the company able to exclude potential risks during production that Pilkington had included in their much higher offer, Vegla proved to be a reliable and innovative partner for the future collaboration and hence was awarded the contract to manufacture the structured glass.

Mike Davies of RRP also attested that using a mock-up had the additional benefit to the ones mentioned above of being a way to find answers. [33] The mock-up was clearly helpful in the search for a formwork system for the beam grid, for which dimensioning by Ove Arup & Partners took an unexpectedly long time. [34] As the dimensioning extended into the mock-up phase, the first mock-up for the formwork systems was produced with beams of different heights. Only after the first mock-up did the beam grid take its final shape. It can be assumed that the construction of the first mock-up with beams of different heights revealed the difficulties for shuttering this form, which was decisive for bringing the beams of the grid to the same height. The impulse to adjust the dimensioning of the beam grid thus originated from a condition which was revealed during construction of the mock-up: 'It was not immediately obvious how to achieve the required quality of concrete finish, consistently, and at times the engineering and architectural development of the grid was a response to our thinking on the formwork system.' [35]

The reconstruction of the mock-up programme for the Lloyd's Building shows that the benefit of mock-ups is twofold: on the one hand, mock-ups can be used to represent things to show and test them; on the other hand, mock-ups can be built to search for expected issues or to find unexpected ones. While the object of investigation is known in the first case, in the second it is assumed that it will be revealed while working on the mock-up. In both cases, insights are gained by using mock-ups to answer known questions and raise new ones. These insights have two effects that form the essential values of mock-ups: they helped promote trust among collaborators and develop buildable constructions.

1   Interview with Mike Davies, 23 March 2016.
2   The team review of mock-ups meetings probably replaced the design progress meetings chaired by Bovis mentioned above.
3   The reconstruction of the mock-up programme is based on unpublished material from the archives of Arup and RSHP (cf. bibliography). Key excerpts are published in Michael Eidenbenz, 'Solving Lloyd's: Zur Rolle von 1:1 Mock-Ups im Bauprozess' (DSc diss., ETH Zurich, 2018).
4   Email from John Young, 18 December 2015.
5   John Thornton, 'Fabrication Research', *Architectural Design* 75, no. 4 (2005), 100–3.
6   Email from John Young, 18 December 2015.
7   Reginald D. Hough and Vincent J. Kelly, Method For Multi-Storied Concrete Construction and Apparatus Therefore, Patent no. 4,272,465, issued 1981.
8   Email from John Young, 18 December 2015.
9   Bovis Construction Limited, 'Report Following Construction Experience of Mock Up Formwork Systems, Proposal for Superstructure Floor Slab', 12 May 1982.
10 'Design Team Meeting Minutes', Archive RSHP. The final decision was made in a design team meeting in which only persons from RRP, Ove Arup & Partners and MDA (not Bovis) were present.
11 Email from John Young, 18 December 2015.
12 Thornton, 'Fabrication Research'.
13 Rogers, Young and Goldschmied, 'New Headquarters for Lloyd's', 47.
14 Colin Davies, 'Putting It Together', *Architectural Review* 180, no. 1076 (1986), 71.
15 Cf. page 169
16 Cf. page 173
17 Cf. page 169
18 Cf. page 31
19 'Pilkington File', Archive RSHP.
20 Email from Klaus Wertz, 3 December 2015.
21 Email from Klaus Wertz, 15 June 2016.
22 Josef Gartner & Co., 'Air Distribution Tests, Test Report', 8 July 1982.
23 Josef Gartner & Co., 'Lloyd's Redevelopment, Element 440, Tests', 1982.
24 A. F. C. Sherrat, ed., *Air Conditioning: Impact on the Built Environment* (London: Hutchinson, 1987), 117.
25 Franc Sodec, 'Integration des Tischauslasses in den 8-Personen-Schreibtisch der Versicherungsgesellschaft Lloyd's, London', March 1981. Archive Krantz.
26 Interview with Friedrich Wagner, December 2016.
27 John Thornton and Martin Hall, 'Lloyd's Redevelopment', *Arup Journal* 17, no. 2 (1982), 7.
28 Brian Waters, 'Lloyd's Takes Shape', *Building* CCXLIV, no. 7290 (1983), 38.
29 'Mock-Ups for Lloyd's', 20.
30 John Young, 'The Use of Mock-Ups to Test Design' (1983).
31 Cf. section 'Embossing the Structured Glass'.
32 Interview with Stephen Le Roith, 23 March 2016.
33 Interview with Mike Davies, 23 March 2016.
34 Cf. section 'Shuttering the Beam Grid'.
35 Thornton, 'Fabrication Research'.

7. Constructing Lloyd's

It takes the learning curve of building away from the site, so that by the time the contractor is on site, each element of the design is a tested and proven system.

John Young 'The Use of Mock-Ups to Test Design' (1983)

7.01 Pre-fabricated toilet capsule being craned into position, finished beam grid in the foreground

7.02 Construction of the column bracket assembly

a In-situ column with reinforcement cast up to the soffit of the bracket
b Pre-fabricated bracket placed over top of column
c Pre-fabricated yoke placed on top of bracket
d Reinforcement of U-beam setup

7.03 Shuttering system in action

a Support for formwork setup
b Soffit formwork with reinforcement support cradles placed
c Reinforcement setup
d Edge formwork, posts for mounting stub columns and support deck setup
e Mounted stub column
f Cast beam grid
g Removed formwork
h Steel permanent formwork panel placed on top of stub columns

7.04 Construction of a floor slab showing different stages of the shuttering process

7.05a–b Finished superstructure of the Room at ground level

7.05c Finished superstructure of the Room at ground level

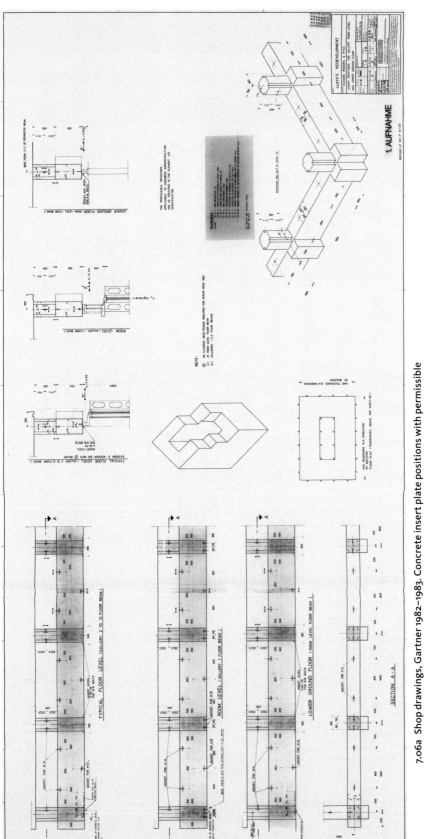

7.06a Shop drawings, Gartner 1982–1983. Concrete insert plate positions with permissible deviations for Gleeson, the superstructure subcontractor

7.06b Shop drawings, Gartner 1982–1983. Facade vertical section, top

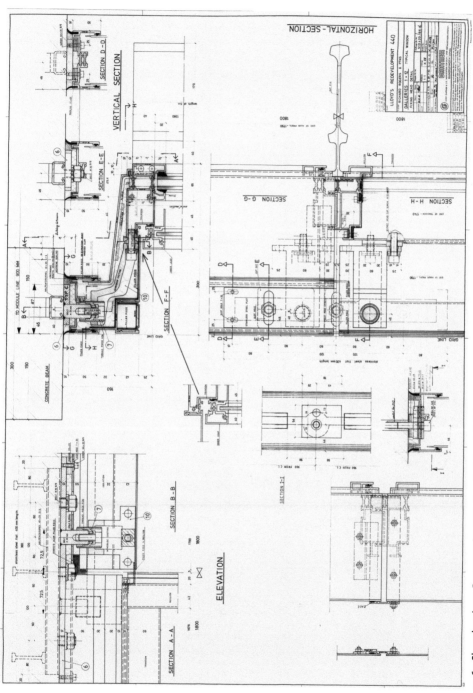

7.06c Shop drawings, Gartner 1982–1983. Facade fixing detail, top

199

7.06d Shop drawings, Gartner 1982–1983. Facade vertical section, bottom

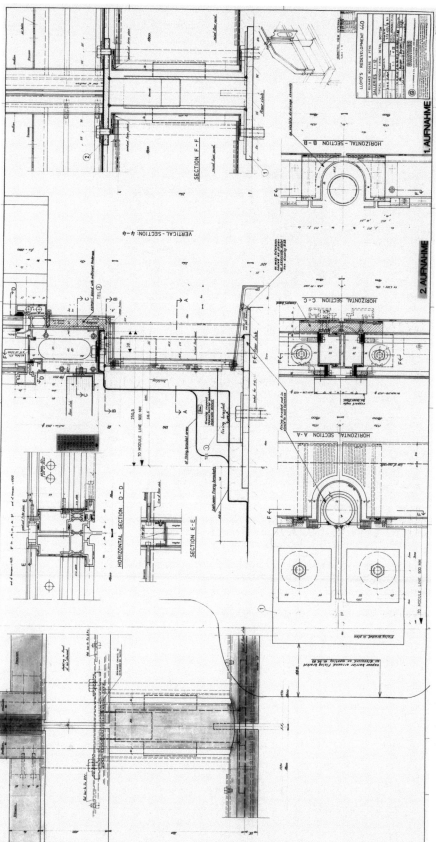

7.06e Shop drawings, Gartner 1982–1983. Facade fixing detail, bottom

7.07 Fixation of the facade [1984?]

a At the top, a fixing bracket made of casted aluminium connects the beam grid and the window elements with hinge joints that can absorb the movements of the structure.

b At the bottom, deviations of the concrete construction can be accommodated with an adjustable mounting foot.

c Finished facade construction

Lloyd's 1:1

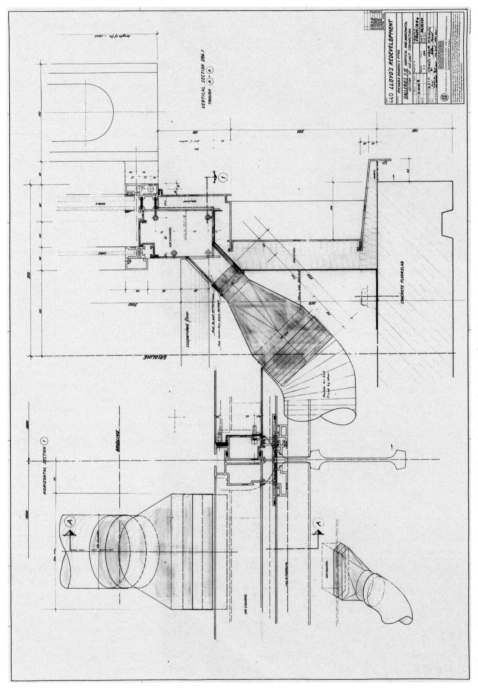

7.06f Shop drawings, Gartner 1982–1983. Vertical and horizontal section of air duct connection

204

7.08 Lower area of the facade cavity with perforation for exhaust air and suction connection [1984?]

7.09 Facade element, inner pane opened

8. Mock-ups: The Currency of Experimenting

> An experimental system is, to use the words of [François] Jacob,
> a 'machine for producing the future'. It allows one to formulate
> the questions one can answer in the first place. It is a device
> for materialising questions.[1]
> Hans-Jörg Rheinberger

Mock-ups made two significant contributions for the building design of the Lloyd's Building: they helped to promote trust and to realise the construction of the building. Although the Lloyd's Building was developed under extraordinary conditions, the insights gained from this research do not depend on them. The decision to use mock-ups in the first place may have benefited from the social and architectural zeitgeist, financial resources and local conditions but their capability remains a fact independent of these.

As a case study, the Lloyd's Building allows greater understanding of the nature of an iterative design process that applied mock-ups as its ultimate design tool. It helped identify strategies to deal with complex design problems. By analysing the role of mock-ups – a role far more significant than assumed at the beginning of this research – we see how mock-ups are not only models; they also function as experiments. They therefore are not only tools to assess the qualities of a proposed building but also instruments to produce knowledge. This sets them apart from virtual design tools which, though very powerful and much more affordable, are limited in their experimental function to the scope of virtual reality. Although mock-ups are an additional expense to the direct costs of construction, ultimately their costs are counterbalanced by their abilities in the long term. When seen as experiments, mock-ups allow architects, contractors and clients to take risks and be open to innovative solutions in the design. This makes them of great value in solving complex building projects and invaluable drivers for the epistemic development of architecture as a discipline.

Mock-Ups as Experiments

Mock-ups can serve to generate both answers and questions and are therefore ideal objects for experimentation. Not only models, they may also function as experiments, similar to the use of experimental systems in the natural sciences. Although architectural mock-ups and scientific experimental systems function the same when it comes to how knowledge is produced, they differ as models in terms of the respective reality they represent. This difference is of consequence to the conditions under which this knowledge is produced.

An experiment consists of two functional entities: the 'epistemic things' that drive the questions and the 'technical objects' that are made to reveal the answers.[2] While an epistemic thing is something vague, the technical object is real and tangible. Together they form a dynamic, ever-evolving system: as soon as epistemic things can be reliably answered by technical objects, they vanish. Technical objects, however, may be questioned and in turn themselves become subjects of research. This 'continued dialectic between epistimicity and technicity'[3] drives experimental systems in science.

As this case of the Lloyd's Building design has shown, mock-ups may function like experimental systems. They can trigger a process of continuous research, over the course of which they are changed by their users to find the answers to questions. As long as the users are open for changes that may reveal the unforeseen, mock-ups are 'machines for creating the future'.[4] Once all questions are answered, mock-ups stabilize and turn into technical systems that can finally be integrated in the construction process.

The technical objects for the beam grid mock-ups in the Lloyd's Building, such as concrete mixes and formwork systems, first had to be identified to produce different mock-ups of the beam grid design. After the first attempts, questions remained about the quality of the concrete and new questions about the process, sequence and accuracy were raised. Only with further tests and with the involvement of Gleeson as a subcontractor could a formwork system and a concrete mix (that is, a technical system) be developed that could be used to build a beam grid that met all requirements. This back and forth between questions and answers is also evident in other issues that were researched with mock-ups, for example in the development of structured glass. During the mock-up programme, the original subject of research thus became more tangible (and in some cases shifted) and was finally stabilised and could be integrated as a technical system in the overall construction process for the Lloyd's Building.

Not all mock-ups for the Lloyd's Building were equally useful for generating answers and questions, however. The measurement logs and reports on the airflow in the exhaust air facade show that this mock-up was primarily to provide answers and not raise questions. The question asked before constructing the mock-up remained fixed during the measurement: At what speed and at what point must the air be guided into the space between the panes of glass so that the specified limit values are maintained? In this case the mock-ups functioned not as experiments but as models to explore the properties of the designed construction.

The quality of the experimental reality represented by architectural mock-ups differs from the one represented by the scientific experiments. In science, that reality is *spatially* outside the observed nature; in architecture, that reality is *temporally* outside the projected building. Science strives to understand the modelled reality: the phenomenon of nature. To predict and control it, architecture aims at creating a modelled reality – a future building – to fulfil a client's needs. While science thus is primarily concerned with producing knowledge, architecture is ultimately about producing an object: the building. Because of the client's interests, architecture is much more subject to economic constrains than science. Clients require guaranties for fulfilling the commissioned project within a given budget and timeframe. While the continuous change of scientific experiments is mainly limited by the curiosity of the researcher and the available technical processes, the evolution of architectural mock-ups is mainly limited by available budget and time.

If mock-ups are applied as experiments, they must be stabilised as technical systems to be integrated into the construction process. The mock-ups for the Lloyd's Building were planned as experiments that could change only during a limited period: all open questions had to be answered before construction. Otherwise, the design team would have been forced to fall back on already known technical systems and compromise Lloyd's request, or the experiment would have continued during building construction and would have jeopardised the building's completion.

As stabilised technical systems, once-experimental mock-ups have become a part of building culture – the collective knowledge on how to solve requirements of the built environment by architectural concept and technological systems. Building culture is a system that serves most building projects to get designed and constructed without the need of major problem solving. As this case study of the Lloyd's Building design has shown, extraordinary requests demanded the framework of building culture to be questioned and expanded. The visionary design of the Lloyd's Building could not be realised with the available technical means, and the local building culture was not considered capable of delivering the desired quality. Yet, a vision must not deviate too much from what the current building culture is able to provide, as the required experimentations are restricted to the project budget and schedule. Architectural mock-ups can therefore be considered experimental systems, but contrary to the ones in science, their evolution is not continuous but discrete from project to project, always bound to the design of an actual building. Even with this limitation, they are experimental systems and, as 'devices to produce scientific innovations that exceed our current knowledge',[5] are indispensable drivers for the further development of a building culture.

Virtual Mock-Ups

Although this case study on the design process of the Lloyd's Building has shown that mock-ups are suitable for developing knowledge for novel designs and building trust for further collaboration, the question remains to be answered of whether mock-ups are still relevant today amidst powerful and affordable virtual design tools.

To grasp and master complex projects in their entirety, the construction industry has been placing great hope in information technology for some time now. With the aid of a shared data structure (referred to more commonly as a building information model) that collects all aspects of a project, from the geometry to physical and chemical properties to costs or construction time, even highly complex projects should become manageable. In addition to sharing information, such data structures can also be used as virtual mock-ups for analysis, simulations and optimisations. Various digital methods promise to handle a wide range of perspectives in real time: for example, code compliance, load-bearing behaviour, energy consumption, environmental impact, construction process and costs. Yet the processing of virtual mock-ups is limited to information that is represented as data, based on explicit, codifiable and formal knowledge. Virtual mock-ups are always self-referential systems – that is, they are self-contained and cannot provide insights that lie outside the scope of their coded virtual reality. When it comes to exploiting tacit knowledge or real experimentation, they fall short – exactly because they are virtual and not real. This limitation does not negate their justifiability for routine examinations or initial clarifications. It is important, however, not to be blinded by their supposedly correct representation of reality. Designers must be aware of the factors that are neglected by virtualisation, including factors that may not even be apparent. After all, even apparently fully controlled virtual models (such as light simulations), which are among the most advanced physical models, are still not comparable alternatives to mock-ups; they are valuable additions to mock-ups. The exact delimitation or the interaction of the two complementary design tools must be evaluated repeatedly. Despite the promises of digital design tools, real mock-ups therefore are still relevant today.

The Value of Architectural Mock-Ups

Mock-ups incur considerable costs (both for companies working on an acquisition basis and for the client who funds the endeavour) without generating a measurable return. Yet economic profit is not suited for valuating mock-ups: although the knowledge and trust that can be gained by mock-ups undoubtedly has a positive impact on the project budget, their value is difficult to quantify and often only becomes visible in later projects when the technical system can be applied again. The decision for or against the use of mock-ups must therefore not be linked to possible profit but must be made independently based on the desired quality, control and perceived responsibility to further develop the building culture.

Mock-ups are not only excellent means of anticipating and planning the construction process, they are also the architect's only means of promoting constructive inventions while minimizing the associated risks and thus triggering innovations in building culture. It can be argued that construction technology is sufficiently advanced for ordinary building tasks and that research should be carried out outside the real project in an academic or industrial setting. In fact, construction industry activity is to a large extent determined by actors who primarily want or need to create value and see no reason to question the status quo of building culture. However, this part of the construction and supply industry is also dependent on development and benefits from knowledge that is generated in other areas that reflect new production conditions. Academic and industrial research, in turn, is a viable way to overcome the economic constraints of construction technology research in the context of a project. In contrast, this case study clearly shows that the tension between the architectural concept and the technical construct generates the driving force necessary to implement inventions and transform them into a construction industry reality. Both the academy and the industry can only do preliminary work in this respect.

In projects where building design is still recognised as an intellectual, creative activity rather than sheer application of standards and rules, the relationship between architecture and the construction industry must inevitably be questioned, relativised and renewed. This further develops building culture, preventing it from freezing into formalism, and promotes the competitiveness of this important branch of the economy. It would seem wise, therefore, for public authorities and institutional investors to promote such projects and for clients to prioritize innovation. Yet an important prerequisite is clarification of the contractual conditions – there are still many obstacles to be overcome, especially in the context of public procurement. Using a mock-up helps architects strengthen their key competence, their ability to innovate in the construction process – a competence they are in danger of losing to the supply industry. The architect, as an experienced generalist, can steer the investigation in the most promising directions and thus act as a researcher and inventor. Experimenting with mock-ups corresponds to a genuine way of working and helps use skills in a more targeted and effective way to work in a process that oscillates between project and product, between *quod significatur et quod significat*.

The experimental nature of the Lloyd's Building mock-ups allowed the client, the architects and the engineers to take risks in the building design. This enabled them to implement the visions of the megastructure and the intelligent environment in their design, two concepts essential for solving Lloyd's requirements for a building that would fulfil its needs for at least fifty years. The solutions found for the construction entered wider construction culture and were applied to or further developed in later projects by other teams. In the case of the Lloyd's Building, the value of architectural mock-ups not only models but also as experiments was demonstrated for not only questioning new approaches but also providing solutions for optimisation. Mock-ups therefore are not only an essential tool for solving complex design problems but also provide important tools for research and drivers for the progress of a building culture that serves the sustainable development of our society. Mock-ups are an architectural currency whose exchange rate has been and will remain high in the future.

1   Hans-Jörg Rheinberger, *Experiment, Differenz, Schrift: Zur Geschichte der Epistemischen Dinge* (Marburg an der Lahn: Basilisken-Presse, 1992), 25.
2   These terms are taken from molecular biologist and historian of science Hans-Jörg Rheinberger, who has described and investigated the nature of experimental systems in science in depth. Cf. Hans-Jörg Rheinberger, *Experiment, Differenz, Schrift: Zur Geschichte Der Epistemischen Dinge* (Marburg an der Lahn: Basilisken-Presse, 1992) and Hans-Jörg Rheinberger, *Toward a History of Epistemic Things: Synthesizing Proteins in the Test Tube* (Stanford: Stanford University Press, 1997).
3   Hans-Jörg Rheinberger, 'Epistemische Dinge – Technische Dinge', 2008, https://vimeo.com/2351486 (accessed 5 March 2021).
4   François Jacob according to Rheinberger, *Experiment, Differenz, Schrift*, 25.
5   Rheinberger, 'Toward a History'.

Bibliography

Unpublished Sources

'Architects Instructions Element 110', 1981–1985. Project J0170, box 234, item 7. Archive RSHP, London.

Bovis Construction Ltd. 'Report Following Construction Experience of Mock Up Formwork Systems, Proposal for Superstructure Floor Slab', 12 May 1982. Project 8787, box 457, F7500015382855. Archive Arup, London.

'Coordination Meeting Minutes', 1980–1981. Project J0170, box 193, item 4 ARC3254. Archive RSHP, London.

'Coordination Meeting Minutes', 1982. Project J0170, box 193, item 2 ARC73526. Archive RSHP, London.

'Design Team Meeting Minutes', 1978–1981. Project J0170, box 193, item 3 ARC3255. Archive RSHP, London.

'Design Team Memos/Information'. Project J0170, box 193, item 1 ARC3527. Archive RSHP, London.

Josef Gartner & Co. 'Air Distribution Tests, Test Report', 8 July 1982. Project 8787, box 601, FM00008843970. Archive Arup, London.

Josef Gartner & Co. 'Lloyd's Redevelopment, Element 440, Tests', 1982. Project 8787, box 601, FM00008843970. Archive Arup, London.

Ove Arup & Partners. 'A Proposal for the Air-Conditioning of the Superstructure', 1980. Project 8787, box 601, FM00008843970. Archive Arup, London.

Piano + Rogers Architects. 'A Design Strategy for Lloyd's', February 1978, ARC82055. Archive RSHP, London.

'Pilkington File', 1978–1982. Project J0170, box 104, item 4, ARC53512. Archive RSHP, London.

Richard Rogers + Partners. 'Lloyd's: Detail Design Development July 1980–March 1982', June 1982, ARC70790. Archive RSHP, London.
—. 'Lloyd's: Outline Proposals Report', June 1979, ARC82059. Archive RSHP, London.
—. 'Lloyd's: Scheme Design Development Report June 1979–June 1980', June 1980, ARC5574. Archive RSHP, London.
—. 'Lloyd's: Tower Capsule, Manufacturing + Fabricators Briefing Guide', December 1979, ARC86484. Archive RSHP, London.

Rogers Patscenter Architects. 'Notes on the Future of Glass', January 1979, ARC70792. Archive RSHP, London.

Sodec, Franc. 'Integration des Tischauslasses in den 8-Personen-Schreibtisch der Versicherungsgesellschaft Lloyd's, London', March 1981. Archive Krantz.

'Team Review of Mock-Ups, Meeting Minutes'. Project 8787, box 183, item M, LIQ1883-2. Archive Arup, London.

'Technical Notes', 1979–1980. Project J0170, box 323, item 1. Archive RSHP, London.

'Technical Notes', 1980–. Project J0170, box 323, item 4. Archive RSHP, London.

Young, John. 'Design Notes', 1979–1980. Project J0170, box 323, item 2 ARC86569. Archive RSHP, London.

Young, John. 'The Use of Mock-Ups to Test Design', September 1983. Archive Young.

Young, John. 'U.S. Trip Itinerary/Notes', 1981. Project J0170, box 323, item 5. Archive RSHP, London.

Publications about the Lloyd's Building

Appleyard, Brian. *The New Lloyd's: A Visitor's Guide*. London: Lloyd's of London, n.d.

'Architecture and the Programme: Lloyd's of London'. *International Architect* 1, no. 3 (1980): 25–39.

Ashworth, Geoffrey. 'Computers Take on the Lloyd's Challenge'. *Building* CCL, no. 7443 (1986): 55–7.

Banham, Reyner. 'The Quality of Modernism'. *Architectural Review* 180, no. 1076 (1986): 53–6.

Barefoot, Jack. 'Lloyd's Room to Last a Hundred Years'. *Concrete* 17, no. 4 (1983): 36–41.

Blackmore, Courtenay. *The Client's Tale: The Role of the Client in Building Buildings*. London: RIBA, 1990.

Boys, Jos. 'Grown Men's Game'. *Architects' Journal* 184, no. 43 (1986): 107–9.

Brown, André. *Peter Rice*. London: Thomas Telford Publishing, 2001.

Buchanan, Peter. 'Foster/Rogers: High-Tech. Classical/Gothic'. *Architectural Review* 169, no. 1011 (May 1981): 265–7.
—. 'Machines for Working In'. *Architectural Review* 180, no. 1076 (1986): 40–2.

Carolin, Peter. 'Two Engineered Solutions'. *Architects' Journal* 184, no. 43 (1986): 78–94.

Castellano, Aldo. 'High-Tech Storico'. *L'Arcaplus* 5, no. 18 (1998): 4–15.

'Conclusion'. *Architects' Journal* 184, no. 44 (1986): 40–5.

Cruickshank, Dan. 'Lloyd's Redevelopment'. *Architectural Review* 169, no. 1011 (May 1981): 277–82.

Davies, Colin. 'Putting It Together'. *Architectural Review* 180, no. 1076 (1986): 69–80.

—. 'Teamwork'. *Architectural Review* 180, no. 1076 (1986): 93.

—. 'The "Omniplatz"'. *Architectural Review* 180, no. 1076 (1986): 59–68.

'Design for Better Assembly: (5) Case Study: Rogers' and Arup's'. *Architects' Journal* 180, no. 36 (1984): 87–94.

Dietsch, Deborah K. 'Lloyd's of London'. *Architectural Record* 11 (1986): 104–17.

Duffy, Frank. 'Between the Diagram and the Detail'. *Architects' Journal* 184, no. 43 (1986): 117–20.

Eidenbenz, Michael. 'Solving Lloyd's: Zur Rolle von 1:1-Mock-Ups im Bauprozess', DSc diss., ETH Zurich, 2018.

Fillion, Odile. 'Contradictions in the City'. *Architecture Interieure Cree* (1986): 74–89.

'Fine Art Praise for "Brilliant" New Lloyd's. *Building Design*, no. 449 (1979): 1, 3.

Fordham, Max. 'Excitement of Services'. *Architectural Review* 180, no. 1076 (1986): 84–8.

Grover, Reginald. 'Lloyd's Lift Logic Is UK Pacesetter'. *RIBA Journal* 91, no. 3 (1984): 36–7.

Hagan, Susan. 'Lloyd's Assured'. *Architects' Journal* 169, no. 23 (1979): 1144–6.

Hannay, Patrick. 'A Tale of Two Architectures'. *Architects' Journal* 184, no. 44 (1986): 29–39.

—. 'Two Politics of Patronage'. *Architects' Journal* 184, no. 43 (1986): 48–74.

Hargreaves, Henry and Max Fordham. 'Dressing up the Duct'. *Building Services: The CIBSE Journal* 8, no. 9 (1986): 60–2.

Heron, Patrick. 'Blue Cranes in the Sky'. *Architectural Review* 180, no. 1076 (1986): 57–8.

Hunt, Anthony. 'Structural Concept'. *Architectural Review* 180, no. 1076 (1986): 83.

Le Roith, Stephen. 'Insight: Glass at Lloyd's. *AJ Focus* (April 1987): 36–9.

'Lloyd's'. *Arup Journal* 21, no. 4 (1986): 22–7.

'Lloyd's and the Bank'. *Architects' Journal* 184, no. 43 (1986): 44–5.

'Lloyd's: Insurance Market, London'. *The Architectural Review* CLXXX, no. 1076 (1986): 43–8.

'Lloyd's of London'. *Techniques & ARCHITECTURE* 350 (1983): 95–100.

'Lloyd's of London'. *Architecture and Urbanism* 198 (1987).

'Lloyd's of London'. *Glasforum* 37, no. 2 (1987): 9–18.

'Lloyd's of London: Detail Design Development'. *Architecture and Urbanism* 198 (1987): 95–118.

'Mock-Ups for Lloyd's'. *Building* CCXLVII, no. 43 (1984): 20.

Morganti, Renato. 'La nuova sede direzionale dei Lloyd's a Londra'. *L' Industria Della Costruzioni* XX, no. 180 (1986): 34–50.

Murray, Peter. 'The Frontiers of Patronage'. *RIBA Journal* 86, no. 9 (1979): 404–8.

Pawley, Martin. 'Into the Unknown'. *Architectural Review* 180, no. 1076 (1986): 88–90.

—. 'Two Triumphs of Twisted Wire'. *Architects' Journal* 184, no. 43 (1986): 113–15.

Powell, Kenneth. *Lloyd's Building*. London: Phaidon, 1994.

—. *Richard Rogers*. 3 vols. Complete Works. London: Phaidon, 1999.

'Projekt für die Lloyd's Versicherer in London'. *Werk, Bauen + Wohnen* 67, no. 4 (1980): 14–27.

'Projet d'immeuble de bureaux pour le Lloyd's'. *L'architecture d'aujourd'hui* 207 (1980): 56–8.

Rice, Peter. *An Engineer Imagines*. London: Artemis, 1994.

—. 'Exploring the Boundaries of Design'. London: Pidgeon Audiovisual, 1986.

Rice, Peter and John Thornton. 'Lloyd's Redevelopment'. *The Structural Engineer* 64A, no. 10 (1986): 265–81.

Roberts, John. 'Sanitary Connections: A Case History of Innovation'. *Arup Journal* 19, no. 3 (1984): 24–7.

Rogers, Richard. 'Genesis of the New Lloyd's Underwriting Room'. London: Pidgeon Audiovisual, 1979.

Rogers, Richard, John Young and Marco Goldschmied. 'New Headquarters for Lloyd's'. *RIBA Transactions* 4, no. 1 (1985): 44–53.

Sherrat, A. F. C., ed. *Air Conditioning: Impact on the Built Environment*. London: Hutchinson, 1987.

Sodec, Franc and Richard Craig. 'The Underfloor Air Supply System: The European Experience'. In *ASHRAE Transactions*, 96 (1990): 690–95.

Spring, Martin. 'Gossip from the Coffee-House'. *Building* CCL, no. 7450 (1986): 38–9.

Stevens, Ted. 'Putting the Tech into Architecture'. *New Scientist* 88, no. 1231 (1980): 704–5.

Stokdyk, John. 'BAS-Relief'. *Building* CCLV, no. 7671 (1990): 63.

Sudjic, Deyan. *The Architecture of Richard Rogers*. London: Wordsearch, 1994.
—. 'The Romance of the Machine'. *Blueprint* 1, no. 25 (1986): 34–7.

Thornton, John. 'Fabrication Research'. *Architectural Design* 75, no. 4 (2005): 100–3.

Thornton, John and Martin Hall. 'Lloyd's Redevelopment'. *Arup Journal* 17, no. 2 (1982): 2–7.

Vernes, Michel. 'Fureur et mystère, la Lloyd's. *Archi Cree* 190 (1982): 108–11.

Wang, Wilfried. 'Edificio Lloyd's'. *Domus*, no. 680 (1987): 25–37.

Waters, Brian. 'A Year at Lloyd's'. *Building* CCXLVII, no. 7361 (1984): 30–7.
—. 'Lloyd's Takes Shape'. *Building* CCXLIV, no. 7290 (1983): 32–8.
—. 'The Inside Story'. *Building* CCXLIX, no. 7425 (1985): 38–41.

Winter, John. 'Comparing Products'. *Architects' Journal* 184, no. 43 (1986): 97–102.

Worthington, John and Rodney Cooper. 'Beyond the City Limits'. *Designers' Journal* 20 (1986): 40–53.

Additional Sources

Appleyard, Bryan. *Richard Rogers: A Biography*. London: Faber & Faber, 1986.

Banham, Reyner. 'A Clip-On Architecture'. *Design Quarterly* 63 (1965): 2–30.
—. 'A Home Is Not a House'. *Art in America* 2 (1965): 70–9.
—. 'Louis Kahn: The Buttery-Hatch Aesthetic'. *The Architectural Review* 131, no. 781 (1962): 203–6.
—. *Megastructure: Urban Futures of the Recent Past*. London: Thames & Hudson, 1976.
—. *New Brutalism: Ethic or Aesthetic?* London: Architectural Press, 1966.
—. 'Piano + Rogers' Architectural Method'. *A+U* 66, no. 6 (1976): 63–7.
—. *The Architecture of the Well-Tempered Environment*. London: Architectural Press, 1969.
—. 'The Services of the Larkin "a" Building'. *Journal of the Society of Architectural Historians* 37, no. 3 (1978): 195–7.
—. *Theory and Design in the First Machine Age*. London: Architectural Press, 1960.

Baudon, Jacques. 'Projet pour le concours de la maison européene'. *Techniques & Architecture* 20, no. 1 (1959): 99.

Blondel, Jacques-François. *Cours d'architecture, ou traité de la décoration, distribution & construction des bâtiments*. 6 vols. Paris: Desaint, 1773.

Brandle, Kurt and Robert F. Boehm. 'Evaluation of Air-Flow Windows: Final Report'. Lawrence Berkeley Laboratory, University of California, 1981.

Brookes, Alan. *Concepts in Cladding*. Harlow: Construction Press (Longman), 1985.
—. *Connections: Studies in Building Assembly*. Oxford: Butterworth Architecture, 1992.

Brookes, Alan and Chris Grech. *The Building Envelope*. London: Butterworth Architecture, 1990.

Bryan, Harvey J. 'Le Corbusier and the "Mur neutralisant": An Early Example in Double Envelope Construction'. In *Architecture and Urban Space*, Servando Alvarez, Jaime Lopes de Asiain, Simos Yannas and E. de Oliveira Fernandes, eds. Dordrecht: Kluwer, 1991.

Campbell Cole, Barbie and Ruth Elias Rogers, eds. *Richard Rogers + Architects*, Architectural Monographs 10. London: Academy Editions, 1985.

Carter, John. 'Management Contracting'. *The Architects' Journal* 156, no. 50 (1972): 1371–4.

'Chrysalis'. *Architectural Design* XLIII (March 1972): 172–74.

Clamp, Hugh, Stanley Cox and Sarah Lupton. *Which Contract?* London: RIBA, 2007.

Clausen, Meredith L. 'Frank Lloyd Wright, Vertical Space, and the Chicago School's Quest for Light'. *Journal of the Society of Architectural Historians* 44, no. 1 (1985): 66–74.

Conolly, Simon, Mike Davies, Johnny Devas, David Harrison and Dave Martin. 'Pneu World'. *Architectural Design* 38, no. 6 (1968): 257–72.

Cook, Peter. 'London Collection'. *Architectural Review* 180, no. 1076 (1986): 49–54.
—. 'The Engineers Intervene'. *The Architectural Review* CLXXIV, no. 1037 (1983): 48–50.

Cooper, Peter. *Building Relationships: The History of Bovis*. London: Cassell, 2000.

Croome, Derek J. 'Building Service Engineering: The Invisible Architecture'. *Building Services Engineering Research and Technology* 11, no. 1 (1990): 27–31.

Davies, Mike. 'A Wall for All Seasons'. *RIBA Journal* 88, no. 2 (1981): 55–7.
—. 'Intelligent Buildings'. Recorded talk. London: Pidgeon Audiovisual, 1987.
—. 'The Design of the Intelligent Environment'. In *High-Tech Buildings*. London: Online Publications, 1986, 159–67.

Duffy, Francis. 'Bürolandschaft '58–'78'. *The Architectural Review* CLXV, no. 983 (1979): 54–8.

Dunn, Nick. *Ecology of the Architectural Model*. Bern: Peter Lang, 2007.

Echenique, Marcial. 'Models: A Discussion'. *Architectural Research and Teaching* 1, no. 1 (May 1970): 25–30.

Gannon, Todd. *Reyner Banham and the Paradoxes of High Tech*. Los Angeles: Getty, 2017.

Hough, Reginald D. and Vincent J. Kelly. Method for Multi-Storied Concrete Construction and Apparatus Therefore. Patent no. 4,272,465, issued 1981.

'House for 1960'. *Architectural Review* 127, no. 758 (1960): 223.

Laing, Nikolaus. 'The Use of Solar and Sky Radiation for Air Conditioning of Pneumatic Structures'. In *Proceedings of the 1st International Colloquium on Pneumatic Structures*, 163–77. Stuttgart: International Association for Shell Structures; Institut für Modellstatik, 1967.

Jarzabkowski, Paula, Gary Burke and Paul Spee. 'Constructing Spaces for Strategic Work: A Multimodal Perspective'. *British Journal of Management* 26 (2015): 26–47.

Maki, Fumihiko. *Investigations in Collective Form*. St. Louis: The School of Architecture, Washington University, 1964.

Makowski, Zygmunt Stanislaw. *Steel Space Structures*. London: Michael Joseph, 1965.

Naoum, Shamil G. and David Langford. 'Management Contracting: The Client's View'. *Journal of Construction Engineering and Management* 113, no. 3 (1987): 369–84.

'Patscentre International: Building Study'. *Architects' Journal* 167, no. 26 (1978): 1247–61.

Piano, Renzo and Richard Rogers. 'Piano + Rogers'. *Architectural Design* 45, no. 5 (May 1975): 275–311.
—. 'Piano + Rogers'. *A+U* 66, no. 6 (1976): 68–122.

Rawstorne, Peter. 'Piano + Rogers: Centre Beaubourg'. *Architectural Design* XLII, no. July (1972): 407–10.

Reuther, Hans and Ekhart Berckenhagen. *Deutsche Architekturmodelle*. Berlin: Verlag für Kunstwissenschaften, 1994.

Rheinberger, Hans-Jörg. 'Epistemische Dinge – Technische Dinge', 2008. https://vimeo.com/2351486 (accessed 5 March 2021).
—. *Experiment, Differenz, Schrift: Zur Geschichte der Epistemischen Dinge*. Marburg an der Lahn: Basilisken-Presse, 1992.
—. *Experimentalsysteme und Epistemische Dinge*. Göttingen: Wallstein Verlag, 2001.

—. *Toward a History of Epistemic Things: Synthesizing Proteins in the Test Tube*. Stanford: Stanford University Press, 1997.

Rogers, Richard. 'Approach to Architecture'. *RIBA Journal* 84, no. 1 (1977): 11–12.
—. 'La "casa di vetro" di Pierre Chareau: Una rivoluzione che non continua.' *Domus* 443, no. 10 (1966): 8–20.
—. 'Observation on Architecture'. In Barbie Campbell Cole and Ruth Elias Rogers, eds. *Richard Rogers + Architects*. Architectural Monographs 10. London: Academy Editions, 1985, 8–19.
—. 'The Artist and the Scientist'. In Deborah Gans, ed. *Bridging the Gap: Rethinking the Relationship of Architect and Engineer; the Proceedings of the Building Arts Forum/New York Symposium Held in April of 1989 at the Guggenheim Museum*. New York: Van Nostrand Reinhold, 1991, 139–55.

Royal Institute of British Architects, ed. *Architects '85: A Guide to RIBA Practices*. London: RIBA, 1985.
—, ed. *Exploring Material: The Work of Peter Rice*. London: RIBA, 1992.

Sadler, Simon. *Archigram: Architecture Without Architecture*. Cambridge, MA: MIT Press, 2005.

Smets, Michael, Paula Jarzabkowski, Gary T. Burke and Paul Spee. 'Reinsurance Trading in Lloyd's of London: Balancing Conflicting-yet-Complementary Logics in Practice'. *Academy of Management Journal* 58, no. 3 (2015): 932–70.

Smithson, Alison. 'How to Recognize and Read Mat-Building'. *Architectural Design* 44, no. 9 (1974): 573–90.

'The Bubble House: A Rising Market'. *Playboy Magazine* 19, no. 4 (1972): 117–19.

Tricker, Robert Ian. 'The Governance of Lloyd's of London'. *Corporate Governance: An International Review* 1, no. 2 (1993): 84–92.

Wermiel, Sarah. 'Norcross, Fuller and the Rise of the General Contractor in the United States in the Nineteenth Century'. In Malcom Dunkeld, ed. *Proceedings of the Second International Congress on Construction History* 3, Exeter: Construction History Society; Short Run Press, 2006, 3297–313.

Whiteley, Nigel. *Reyner Banham: Historian of the Immediate Future*. Cambridge, MA: MIT Press, 2002.

Wilcoxen, Ralph. *A Short Bibliography on Megastructures* 66. Exchange Bibliography. Monticello: Council of Planning Librarians, 1968.

Image Credits

1.01 © Museen der Stadt Nürnberg / Dokumentationszentrum Reichsparteitagsgelände

1.02 Max Bill, ed. *Robert Maillart: Bridges and Constructions*, 3rd ed. New York: Frederick A. Praeger, 1969: 160.

1.03 Collection Museum Wien

1.04 © Stichting Kröller-Müller Museum, Otterlo, the Netherlands

1.05 © Eva Jiřičná / Royal Collection Trust

1.06 © Richard Bryant / Arcaid

1.07 © Alastair Hunter / RIBA Collections

2.01a © Martin Charles / RIBA Collections

2.01b Brian Appleyard, *The New Lloyd's: A Visitor's Guide*. London: Lloyd's of London, n.d.: 5.

2.02 https://commons.wikimedia.org/wiki/File:Microcosm_of_London_Plate_049_-_Lloyd%27s_Subscription_Room.jpg

2.03 © RSHP / RSHP Archive

2.04 Science Museum Group

2.05 John Young, 'GRC 1: Properties'. *The Architects' Journal* 167, no. 7 (1978): 311–16, here 311.

2.06 Alan Stanton, 'Le bureau du futur'. *Techniques & Architecture* 337 (1981): 66–69, here 68.

2.07a–d, 2.08, 2.09a–b © RSHP / RSHP Archive

3.01 *Municipal Journal*, March 1956.

3.02 'House for 1960'. *Architectural Review* 127, no. 758 (1960): 223.

3.03 © Archigram 1964

3.04 © 2021 François Dallegret, ProLitteris, Zurich

3.05 Simon Conolly et al., 'Pneu World', *Architectural Design* 38, no. 6 (1968): 257–72, here 268.

3.06 Eric Holding, *Mark Fisher: Staged Architecture*. London: Wiley-Academy, 2000. Courtesy of Mike Davies.

3.07 'Chrysalis'. *Architectural Design* XLIII, no. March (1972): 172–74, here 173. Courtesy of Duncan Davies.

3.08 and 3.09 Mike Davies, 'A Wall for All Seasons'. *RIBA Journal* 88, no. 2 (1981): 55–57, here 57. Courtesy of Mike Davies.

4.01a–b, 4.02 © RSHP / RSHP Archive

4.03 J.W. Taylor, photographer. Digital File # 199303_120913_042. J.W. Taylor Photograph Collection, Ryerson and Burnham Art and Architecture Archives, The Art Institute of Chicago.

4.04a–b, 4.05 © RSHP / RSHP Archive

4.06 Reyner Banham, 'Louis Kahn: The Buttery-Hatch Aesthetic'. *The Architectural Review* 131, no. 781 (1962): 203–206, here 205.

4.07 Kisho Kurokawa, *Kisho Kurokawa*. Paris: Editions du Moniteur, 1982: 93.

4.08, 4.09, 4.10a–b, 4.11a–g, 4.12 © RSHP / RS HP Archive

4.13 © Arup / Archive Arup

4.14a–b © RSHP / RSHP Archive

4.15 © John Donat / RIBA Collections

4.16a–b © RSHP / RSHP Archive

4.17a–b, 4.18a–c © Arup / Archive Arup

4.19a–f, 4.20, 4.21, 4.22a–d, 4.23a–b, 4.24, 4.25a–e, 4.26a–c, 4.27 © RSHP / RSHP Archive

4.28, 4.29 © Arup / RSHP Archive

4.30 Richard Rogers, 'La casa di vetro di Pierre Chareau: Una rivoluzione che non continua', *Domus* 443 (October 1966): 8–20, here 13.

4.31, 4.32a–b © RSHP / RSHP Archive

4.33, 4.34 © RSHP Archive

4.35 Reyner Banham, *The Architecture of the Well-Tempered Environment*. London: Architectural Press, 1969: 161.

4.36, 4.37a–b © RSHP / RSHP Archive

4.38a–c © RSHP Archive

4.39, 4.40 © RSHP / Stephen Le Roith Archive

4.41a–b, 4.42 © Arup / Archive Arup

4.43a–c, 4.44, 4.45, 4.46 © RSHP / RSHP Archive

5.03 Peter Cooper, *Building Relationships: The History of Bovis*. London: Cassell, 2000: 50.

5.04 © Mike Abrahams

5.05 Courtenay Blackmore, *The Client's Tale: The Role of the Client in Building Buildings*. London: RIBA, 1990.

5.06, 5.07 © RSHP / RSHP Archive

5.08 © Arup / Archive Arup

6.01 © RSHP / Stephen Le Roith Archive

6.02 © Arup / Archive Arup

6.03, 6.04, 6.05 © RSHP / RSHP Archive

6.06 Archive Arup

6.07 Reginald Hough and Vincent Kelly, Method for Multi-Storied Concrete Construction and Apparatus Therefore, Patent no. 4,272,465, issued 1981.

6.08a © RSHP / Stephen Le Roith Archive

6.08b Archive Arup

6.08c Archive Arup

6.09a–b Archive Arup

6.10a © RSHP / Stephen Le Roith Archive

6.10b–6.10c Archive Arup

6.11 © RSHP / Stephen Le Roith Archive

6.12 © Arup / Archive Arup

6.13, 6.14a–f, 6.15a–f © RSHP / RSHP Archive

6.16a–e, © Gartner / Josef Gartner GmbH Archive

6.17 © RSHP / Stephen Le Roith Archive

6.18a–e © Gartner / Josef Gartner GmbH Archive

6.19a–b, 6.20a © RSHP / Stephen Le Roith Archive

6.20b, 6.21, 6.22, 6.23, 6.24, 6.25 © RSHP / RSHP Archive

6.26, 6.27 © RSHP / Stephen Le Roith Archive

6.28 © RSHP / RSHP Archive

6.29 RSHP Archive

6.30 Raymond McGrath and A. C Frost, *Glass in Architecture and Decoration*. London: The Architectural Press, 1937: 601.

6.31a–b, 6.32 © RSHP / RSHP Archive

6.33, 6.34 RSHP Archive

6.35 © RSHP / RSHP Archive

6.36a–b © Klaus Wertz / Archive Klaus Wertz

6.37 © RSHP / RSHP Archive

6.38 © Gartner / Josef Gartner GmbH Archive

6.39 © RSHP / Stephen Le Roith Archive

6.40 © Gartner / Archive Arup

6.41 © RSHP / RSHP Archive

6.42 © Gartner / Archive Arup

6.43 © Gartner / Josef Gartner GmbH Archive

6.44, 6.45 © Gartner / Archive Arup

6.46a–c © Arup / Archive Arup

6.47a–b © Krantz / Archive Krantz

6.48 © Arup / Archive Arup

6.49 © RSHP / Stephen Le Roith Archive

6.50 © Lighting Design Austria / Lighting Design Austria Archive

6.51, 6.52 © RSHP / RSHP Archive

6.53a–b © Lighting Design Austria / Lighting Design Austria Archive

7.01, 7.02a–d, 7.03a–h, 7.04, 7.05a–c © RSHP / RSHP Archive

7.06a–f © Gartner / Josef Gartner GmbH Archive

7.07a–c © RIBA Collections

7.08, 7.09 © Max Fordham LLP / RIBA Collections

Acknowledgements

The basis for this publication was laid by a doctoral thesis written under the supervision of Sacha Menz at the Chair of Architecture and Building Process at ETH Zurich. My thanks therefore go first and foremost to Sacha Menz, who opened my eyes to the manifolded subject of the design and construction process and who supported me throughout my work in many different ways. Next, I would like to thank Markus Peter, professor of architecture and constrction at ETH Zurich, for his willingness to accompany my dissertation as a co-examiner. I have benefited from his methodological understanding and his profound knowledge at the interface between architecture, construction and technology.

In relation to the case study, the Lloyd's Building, my thanks go to the owner Gaw Capital, in particular Silvia Lee and One Lime Street Company Ltd., who granted me access to the archives. In particular, I am indebted to Rogers Stirk Harbour + Partners, Arup and Josef Gartner, who opened their archives to me for this work. Here my thanks go to Karen Firmin-Cooper, Aymée Thorne Clarke, Peter Mpanga, Chris Luebkemann and Monika Niklaser. I would like to thank Stephen Le Roith, Mike Davies, John Young, Ann Dalzell, Andy Sedwick, Eugen Seefried, Friedrich Wagner, Helmut Regvart, Detlef Makulla and Klaus Wertz for their valuable discussions and correspondence on the planning of the Lloyd's Building. Their explanations, insights and stories have contributed to the richness of this work.

This book would not have been published without the help of the people at the gta Verlag, particularly Jennifer Bartmess, who edited and translated the text, Philippe Mouthon, who did the graphic design, and Ulla Bein and Moritz Gleich. For reviewing the text, I would like to thank Rainer Egloff and Matthew Wells.

Finally, this book was only possible thanks to the moral and organisational support of Katrin König. My deepest thanks goes to her.

Translation, copy-editing and project management
Jennifer Bartmess

Proofreading
Jacqueline Taylor

Graphic concept, typesetting and design
Philippe Mouthon

Image editing and printing
Offsetdruckerei Karl Grammlich GmbH, Pliezhausen

Binding
IDUPA Schübelin GmbH, Owen (Teck)

Fonts
Kievit and Arnhem

Paper
Munken Polar 120 g/m²

© 2021
gta Verlag, ETH Zurich
Institute for the History and Theory of Architecture
Department of Architecture
8093 Zurich, Switzerland
www.verlag.gta.arch.ethz.ch

The series 'Architectural Knowledge' is published by the Department of Architecture and the Institute for the History and Theory of Architecture, ETH Zurich.

© Texts: by the author
© Illustrations: by the image authors and their legal successors; for copyrights, see the credits

Every reasonable attempt has been made by the authors, editors and publishers to identify owners of copyrights. Should any errors or omissions have occurred, please notify us.

The entire contents of this work, insofar as they do not affect the rights of third parties, are protected by copyright. All rights are reserved. No part of this publication may be reproduced, stored in a retrieval system, or transmitted, in any form or by any means, electronic, mechanical, photocopying, recording, or otherwise, without the written permission of the publisher.

Bibliographic information published by the Deutsche Nationalbibliothek
The Deutsche Nationalbibliothek lists this publication in the Deutsche Nationalbibliografie; detailed bibliographic data are available on the Internet under http://dnb.dnb.de.

ISBN 978-3-85676-412-8

gta Verlag
ETH *zürich*